# RECIPES
## *from an*
# ITALIAN
# FARMHOUSE

# RECIPES
## *from an*
# ITALIAN
# FARMHOUSE

## VALENTINA HARRIS

Special photography by
Linda Burgess

CONRAN OCTOPUS

*For Diana with infinite thanks and fondest love*

This edition published 1989 by
Conran Octopus Limited
37 Shelton Street
London WC2H 9HN

This paperback edition published
in 1993 by Conran Octopus Limited

Project Editor – Lorraine Dickey
Editors – Pepita Aris, Scott Ewing
Art Director – Mary Evans
Designer – Christine Wood
Picture Research – Nadine Bazar
Production – Julia Golding
Photographic Stylist – Debbie Patterson
Painted tiles – Barbara Mullarney Wright
Line Artwork – Penny Lovelock
Editorial Assistant – Elizabeth Brooks

British Library Cataloguing in Publication Data
Harris, Valentina
Recipes from an Italian farmhouse
1. Food: Italian dishes. Recipes
I. Title
641.5945

ISBN 1-85029-507 7

Typeset by Elite Typesetting Techniques, Southampton
Printed and bound in Hong Kong

# CONTENTS

# THE BASIC INGREDIENTS

THIS BOOK IS ABOUT ITALIAN COOKERY of the most rustic and uncomplicated sort. The recipes are for the most part classic and traditional family favourites with more than a hint of nostalgia. Italian cooking has its origins firmly embedded in Italy's history of poverty and peasant farming, and these are the dishes that rose directly out of such circumstances.

As a matter of course, I have adapted these very old recipes for use on modern cookers. Not many of us have the facilities that the originators of the dishes would have had, for example, the embers of a real wood fire, in which to leave the casserole on a slow cook for almost a night or a day. Although these dishes are born of the simplest life imaginable, it is a simplicity rich in the best that nature has to offer. If you observe the rules, and use the freshest herbs, good quality olive oil and patient cooking, then you will taste the dishes in their true essence.

When vegetables are grown in small quantities, as is the practice on Italian small-holdings, with plenty of good old-fashioned organic manure, they have a flavour worlds removed from plastic wrapped, mass-produced vegetables. National differences do have to be taken into account – some tomatoes, for example, have nothing like the flavour of their Italian counterparts, and you may have to give them a little help with a dab of tomato paste. But this is all in the spirit of peasant cookery, which is anything but a precise art.

It is worth pointing out here that there is no such thing as generic 'Italian' cooking: the cooking of my country is absolutely and obviously regional. What is enjoyed in snow-bound Friuli will quite literally be spat upon under the burning skies of arrogant Calabria. In the book I have included recipes from the length and breadth of the geographical 'boot', including the islands, to give you some inkling of how different the dishes are depending upon where they originate. This is done in no particular order, so you will jump from north to south and east to west. But all the recipes illustrate the need for thrift and a flair for stretching the available ingredients, and this is exactly what made them popular in the first place.

Eating is a ritual in Italy, a very special moment when the family gathers together, where an extra place will always be set for the unexpected visitor. This is not food for 'making an impression', it is everyday *real* food which can be afforded by almost anybody. I have no time for fussy cooking which pretends to the exactness of a chemical equation – for me cooking is essentially intuitive. With a little care and love I like to cook the food which evolved out of necessity, availability and hunger – but which tastes as good now as it did then, food which will feed your body and soul and won't make a bottomless hole in your wallet. Perhaps it is time that we all began to adapt our cooking habits slightly, and chose foods that are as honest and genuine as the fields and the sea. For all these reasons, I am delighted to be able to bring you this very much loved side of the cooking of my Italy.

BUON APPETITO!
Valentina Harris

# CHEESE

Cheese has been a basic dish on the poorest tables for centuries. Italy boasts more varieties of cheese than even France, much of it still craft-made – the flavour reflecting its place of origin. Many excellent cheeses are exported and are easily obtainable in delicatessens and supermarkets.

## PARMESAN

Parmigiano reggiano, made in Emilia Romagna is the most famous of the grana cheeses, which mature to be very grainy and hard and are therefore used for grating. Grana padano is a very similar cheese made in Lombardy, with its name stamped repeatedly over the hard rind.

Parmesan is one of Italy's oldest cheeses. It's also the biggest and the longest matured. It is made from skimmed cows' milk in a big wheel – the whole cheese weighing at least 24 kg (52 lb). As a general rule, the older the cheese, the more expensive it will be. Parmigiano stravecchio is aged a minimum of 2 years. Parmesan is so hard that a wedge-shaped knife is used to split rather than cut the cheese, leaving untidy rough-hewn lumps. Buy these rather than ready-grated cheese, which quickly loses flavour.

Young Parmesan is delicious eaten in hunks with raw young vegetables, but it is most famous as a condiment. It should be sprinkled over the dish after cooking, rather than included in a sauce. A good Parmesan has a granular, even texture and a slight pineapple taste.

## PECORINO

Pecorino is a pungent sheeps' milk cheese produced in every province of the centre and south. It matures more quickly than Parmesan – becoming hard in about 8 months – so in Italy it is considerably cheaper than Parmesan. It is popular for both grating and cooking.

Pecorino romano is well-liked for its pepper flavour, while the Sardinian pecorino sardo is slightly sharp. These cheeses weigh 1.5–4 kg (3–8lb) and have a distinctive 'humpback' shape. The inside is always dense and straw-coloured, while the rind is a guide to age – yellowish when young through to reddish-black.

## PROVOLONE AND CACIOCAVALLO

A familiar cheese from southern Italy, provolone comes in many fanciful shapes, often indented by the strings that contain it. The large oval, from which it derives its name, is the most common type: these can be a metre or more long.

It is a pasta filata cheese, which means that the curds are stretched out in long strips, then bundled together in layers. It should be white or pale straw-coloured and it may develop moist holes when mature. Three main kinds are produced: mild (dolce), sharp (piccante) and smoked (affumicato).

Made in much the same way, caciocavallo are linked in pairs like saddle-bags, which explains their Italian name ('a cavallo' means 'on horseback'). They are kneaded in warm water and shaped by hand.

## STRACCHINO

Stracchino is a generic name for the summer cheeses, a group of cows' milk cheeses made in North Italy (particularly Lombardy and Piedmont), from tired cows, and therefore from thin milk. They are semi-soft and delicate, maturing quickly.

Crescenza is rindless and the softer version is slightly wet, sold wrapped in paper. Gorgonzola is a crescenza, which has blued and matured, and so can be used for melting on food or coated and fried.

The square Taleggio is best known as one of the oldest soft cheeses. It has a soft rosy rind and the taste is more mature than crescenza.

## MOZZARELLA

Mozzarella is a native of Campania, where water buffaloes were introduced in the 16th century. Buffalo milk cheeses are still exported, but are becoming increasingly rare, even in Italy, and cow's milk ones are the norm. It is a fresh, wet cheese, low in fat, sold packed in its own whey, which may be part of the weight given on the packet. Like provolone, it is a pasta filata cheese, made from long strips of curd, cut and wrapped in little bundles – mozzata means cut. Standard sizes are: 125–150 g (4–5 oz) and 250 g (7–9 oz).

Mozzarella is forever associated with pizza – and beloved by Italians – because of the way it binds other ingredients together when it melts.

## RICOTTA

A soft, creamy-looking, fresh ewe's milk cheese, made from the whey, so low in fat, ricotta is identifiable by the mark on its sides of the basket in which it is traditionally drained. It has a crumbly texture and a rich, bland flavour, brought out by cooking.

It is a favourite for pasta stuffings and also for cheesecakes. Half and half cream cheese and cottage cheese makes a passable substitute.

# SALUMI

Salumi means preserved meat – the equivalent of the French charcuterie – all those pork products that are eaten sliced. There are almost as many ways of preserving pork in Italy as there are cheeses. Most of them, like the bacons and salami, keep well. But a few, like Coppa Senese, for which I have given a recipe, and cotechino, described below, though preserved, should be eaten within 3 days.

## HAM

Ham is prosciutto and although Italy does produce cooked ham, called prosciutto cotto, raw ham is so famous that the word by itself means raw ham. Prosciutto is cured by salting and then air-dried. For eating immediately it is carved into the thinnest possible slices, though for cooking it may be cubed.

Parma ham – possibly the world's most famous ham – is the best-known prosciutto crudo and is slightly sweet. San Daniele ham is less sweet and also leaner. The curing process is a long one, the meat of the best quality, and so it is always expensive, particularly from the bone.

## BACON

Pancetta is the salted raw belly of pork, exactly the same cut as bacon. Pancetta arrotolata is commonest abroad, shaped like a long sausage, with the fat belly wrapped round the lean back meat. Some pancetta is smoked – affumicata. Pancetta is the basis of many Italian dishes, cubes being fried with onions and probably other vegetables and herbs, until the onion softens. It's used so often that this 'soffritto' is often just listed as an ingredient in Italian recipe books.

Streaky bacon can be substituted (though bacon in northern Europe contains water, unlike pancetta), or cubed fat cut from ham or gammon.

Guanciale is a speciality from Latium round Rome. It is the pig's cheek – the same cut as a Bath chap in Britain. Bacon is the usual substitute.

## SALAMI

These preserved sausages are made all over the country and in innumerable different local forms. The firm, pinkish-red ones, flecked with white fat, are a familiar sight, but in some parts of Italy the salami meat is soft and is kept in jars covered with lard. Firm salami keep well hanging up, but they should be eaten once cut.

Bologna's famous mortadella is much copied and is said to take its name from the mortar in which the meat was ground. The pink lean pork is ground extremely finely, flavoured with peppercorns and garlic, and then dotted with the white of lard strips, which run down the sausage. Big mortadelle can be as much as 40 cm (16 in) across and are proportionately long.

Salame milano is probably the most popular sausage outside Italy. The texture is fine and some include beef as well as pork. As a general rule, the further south you go, the more highly seasoned the salami – salami di Napoli include chillies. Cacciatore are a rather hard, small salami bought whole. Another huge one is finocchiona, whose name refers to the wild fennel with which it is flavoured.

In Italy look for casalingo, which are the farm-made salami; they are usually coarser than mass-produced ones, but inspire as much connoisseurship as the cheeses. A few are sold abroad under regional names.

## COTECHINO

Cotechino is a preserved meat which nevertheless should be cooked soon after purchase. It contains lean meat from the head and neck of the pig, well spiced, but the most important constituent is chopped, salted pork rind. With slow cooking this fat becomes jellied and oozes out when the sausage is cut. For this reason it is always served with lentils, boiled potatoes or beans to soak up the fat.

To cook, prick it in several places with a fork, wrap in a cloth and boil for 2–3 hours. Cotechino cotto is pre-cooked and sold as boil-in-the-bag. This keeps very well for long periods, then only takes 20 minutes to cook.

## COOKING FATS

Butter used to be confined to Lombardy, near the French border. Traditionally the basic cooking fat comes from beneath the pig's skin, particularly from places without olive trees.

It is sold as salted pork fat, lardo, which keeps, or melted down, called strutto. Now in these cholesterol-conscious days there is a shift to olive oil or to oil pressed from sunflower seeds, girasole.

Olive oil is the base of Southern farmhouse cookery. It is also relatively low on cholesterol and high on minerals. The further south you go, the richer and stronger it becomes.

There are four qualities of oil: second pressing oil is not worth bothering about – it was once used for lighting the street-lamps! A pure, virgin olive oil is exactly what it says it is – and will be sufficient for the recipes in this book.

A greenish, strong, fruity extra vergine is best suited for salads. Superfino oil is the top class and retails at wine prices!

# STARCHES

Italians are accustomed to get their carbohydrates in much more varied ways than just the choice of potatoes or bread eaten further north.

## PASTA

Pasta comes in an infinite variety of forms, but its ingredients are utterly simple – flour and water – sometimes with added oil. Dried pasta is made from durum wheat – the hardest sort – and consequently is more nutritious. Only one traditional pasta – bigoli – is made with wholewheat. Home-made pasta is always made with plain flour, because it is easier to roll this very thinly. Eggs are sometimes added to give richness, when it becomes pasta all 'uovo. The old peasant rule was a 1 egg quantity per person – too much for us now!

In many Italian towns, and now in Italian delicatessens abroad they make and sell fresh pasta on a daily basis. However, once you acquire the knack, it is not difficult to make at home. All the pasta recipes in this book tell you how to make your own pasta – because it is the traditional way, and also because it is light and delicious. (But dried pasta can be substituted for most of the recipes).

Despite its association with Italy as a whole, pasta is the staple of the south of Italy, where it has been the food of the poor for more than two centuries.

The secret of cooking pasta is to use large quantities of boiling water. Drain and serve it the moment it is al dente – still with a little bite. There are three main ways of serving it. In Pasta Asciutta a plain pasta is dressed with a sauce, and the sauces I have given could be used with dried pasta. A pasta in brodo is a fine plain pasta or a delicately stuffed pocket, cooked for a few minutes in a broth. Pasta al forno is baked in layers in a sauce.

## COUSCOUS

Like pasta, Cuscusa is made from durum wheat. Sicilian peasants make it in the classic way, by rolling together two varieties of semolina. You can also buy North African dried couscous, which must be steamed for the same time. Easiest of all is the instant couscous: 500 g (1lb 2 oz) needs soaking in 600 ml (1 pint) boiling water for 10 minutes. Then it should be set over a low heat and fresh broth stirred in.

## RICE

What pasta is to the South, so rice is to Northern Italian cooking. It was introduced by the Saracens and has been cultivated in Lombardy since the 14th century. Spanish rulers then introduced paella and from this evolved Italy's most famous rice dish, risotto.

For risotto there is really no substitute for the large, round-grained rices of Piedmont, Lombardy and the Veneto (which will absorb twice their volume of broth). There are four grades of Italian rice, but fino and superfino are best for risotto, because they keep their shape and firmness during slow cooking. Arborio superfino is sold outside Italy, but vialone, roma and carnaroli are difficult to find. Round grain, ordinario, rice also grows on the Po and is best for puddings.

American long-grain rices can be used for risotto, if you have no choice, but the results will not be the same because they are washed to keep the grains separate after cooking. In a risotto regular stirring encourages the rice to become starchy and bind together.

## POLENTA

Polenta is the Italian name for both the flour that we know as cornmeal and the dish made from it. Dried maize is ground into meal which may be either coarse, medium or fine. It may also be yellow or white – the latter is preferred for fish. For three hundred years it has been the staff of life in much of Lombardy and all of northern Venetia.

To make polenta, the cornmeal is trickled into salted boiling water and stirred over a low heat, until a thick porridge is formed. The amount of water is given on the packet and varies by brand, but usually 450 g (1 lb) absorbs 1.8 litres (3 pints). This takes 30–40 minutes according to brand – cheaper polentas, sold loose, take longer. The polenta is ready when it clings to the spoon and comes away from the side of the pan. In northern Italy traditionally a special pan is kept for it, a copper paiuolo, without the usual tin lining.

The polenta can be served just as it is, or left to set and then baked like lasagne. It is commonly fried to serve as an accompaniment.

## BREAD

Many Italian recipes use home-baked bread as a base, economically employing leftovers before they stale. Soups are poured over bread, slices and crumbs are used for stuffing, and a delicious dolce is made from leftover bread and candied fruit.

Crostini are toasts for topping, while bruschetta is served as an accompaniment. Made of slices of coarse white bread baked in the oven until crisp and golden – or on a charcoal grill – they are rubbed with garlic then anointed with a little olive oil. Pizza, bread baked complete with a tasty sauce, is the pride of the south.

# PULSES AND GRAINS

Pulses and all sorts of other dried vegetables are the staples of the winter kitchen in peasant communities.

## BEANS

For centuries, fagioli or beans have provided farmers with a good source of protein. Fresh beans have vitamins as well, and are preferred for their taste, but dried provide security for the winter months.

Traditionally, beans were softened by soaking overnight with a pinch of bicarbonate of soda. Nowadays this is considered unhealthy, and soaking for an hour in boiling water is preferred.

Dried beans are always brought to the boil and boiled hard for a few minutes before simmering, because it has been discovered that red beans, in particular, contain a harmful enzyme that is not killed by simmering at low temperatures. One to $1\frac{1}{2}$ hours is needed for modern strains of dried beans, which cook somewhat faster than older varieties. Salt is not supposed to be added until the end, because it hardens the beans. Nowadays soup will probably contain 50 g (2 oz) per person, with other vegetables: for a peasant dish this would be doubled.

The best-known type of kidney bean is borlotti; it's always speckled red, on a background that can be anything from pink to dark red. These are frequently cooked with a ham bone, pancetta or some pickled or fresh pork belly.

The handsome white cannellini beans (shown on page 32) are a Tuscan speciality. They can be small or larger, but are always elongated — haricot beans can be substituted. In general different varieties of kidney bean are interchangeable in recipes.

Because of their tough skins, though, dried broad beans are an exception to this rule. These fave are an important food in the south of Italy.

## CHICK PEAS

Ceci are used in Italy in thick soups and even for a pasta sauce. They are often cooked with pork fat in some form, because their mealy texture provides the perfect foil. One of the oldest examples is Ceci con la zampina di maiale (page 70).

Soak chick peas like pulses. Cooking times can vary quite widely by brand, from 30 minutes to more than an hour. Surprisingly the larger ones cook fastest, because these come from strains improved by modern cultivation. (No salt should be used.)

## MAIZE

Introduced in the 17th century, maize is known as granoturco, 'Turkish corn'. Ground to polenta, it became a staple, while dried maize was also stewed.

Nowadays dried maize is either chicken feed or made into popcorn. The latter is useless for stewing in traditional recipes because it has an extremely hard outer skin, designed to hold it together until it explodes, so I have substituted kernels of fresh corn.

# NUTS

Peasants appreciate what is free and the walnut, noce, grows throughout the country. The traditional walnut sauces, with bread, are now used mainly as stuffings.

Almonds, mandorle, make stuffings and are ground for thickening sauces and soups. But the use of almonds for dolce — often very sweet — is an Eastern Mediterranean legacy.

## CHESTNUTS

Chestnuts, castagne, used to be a staple food in the north of Italy, where there are still several cooked dishes. They were also dried and ground to make flour and a predecessor of polenta. Nowadays chestnut flour is used for cakes like Castagnaccio. Better Italian delicatessens stock it in winter and spring, for it has a short shelf life. It can be made by grinding dried nuts, then sifting the results.

## PINE NUTS

Pine kernels, pinoli or pignoli, are extracted from the huge cones of the umbrella pine. These slender cream-coloured little nuts have a unique flavour, slightly aromatic, at once astringent and rich.

# SPICES

After the fresh lemon, always on the tree outside her door, the farmer's wife favours the following two spices.

## JUNIPER BERRIES

Juniper berries, ginepro, are little blue-black fruit with an aromatic-bitter taste, related to pine. Italian juniper is far stronger than that found further north and flavours meat and liqueurs.

## CINNAMON

Rolled cinnamon bark, or cannella, can be ground to a powder at home. In Italy it is used for meat and game as well as the more usual sweet dishes.

# MEAT, POULTRY AND GAME

Poorer households make do without much fresh meat. The highlight of the year is the autumn pig slaughter, which provides fresh maiale (pork) briefly, and a series of salumi for storing. Spicy fresh sausages, salsicce, are common.

Manzo, beef, is eaten more in the north of the country than the south. Better cuts of both beef and veal are used economically, for example to flavour a sauce.

Lambs are often killed at the beginning of summer and I have included several shepherds' recipes for lamb, some using the expensive cuts.

## OFFAL

Please, please don't skip this. There is a tendency to regard offal as a food which the poor ate out of necessity — they did — and think it can now be discarded. This is not so. Many innards and extremities have special qualities or textures which still make them kitchen delicacies. The traditional recipe for calf's head pays for the effort it may take to find the meat.

Italy is proud of its fegato, liver dishes. Tuscany is known for both pigs' liver and its chicken livers, which are very large. But best of all is calves' liver with an exquisite texture.

Sweetbreads, animelle, are less well known, but prized for their perfect white and delicate texture. Each animal has two, one from the throat and one nearer the heart and they are usually sold as a pair. Peel off the membrane, soak for three hours in cold water, then blanch them.

Tripe, trippa, is the animal's stomach lining. As cows, in particular, have several stomachs there are different types: honeycomb tripe is agreed to be the best.

Buy calves' tripe if you can, but you may well find that the only tripe on sale is from a much older animal which needs blanching and scraping, and far longer cooking. However, it is invariably sold 'dressed', that is prepared and three-quarters cooked. It can then be finished following the recipe for a younger animal.

Trotters, zampone, were prized for the way that long cooking turns the rind into a meat jelly. To soak up the juices they are traditionally cooked with pulses or chick peas.

## CHICKEN

Pollo, the barnyard fowl, scratched for her living or ate the same dried maize that fed the poor farmer's family. Buy a free-range or corn-fed (that is maize-fed) chicken. The latter are yellow in colour and so are easy to spot.

## GAME

Wild rabbits, coniglio, caught after feeding on the erbe odorose, wild herbs, taste much better than our tame bunnies — their white meat is very good. Hare, lepre, is popular in northern Italy and Tuscany, but my recipe is from the south.

The Italians have always been fanatic hunters, as the clattering of gunshot in season will testify. Pheasant, duck and songbirds are all targets. My recipe for pigeon on the spit represents a tradition of game barbecued outdoors.

I have not included any recipes for boar because it is hard to get hold of, but it deserves a mention. There used to be lots in the forests around Lucca: they have the gamiest of all game flavours, and are extremely chewy.

# FISH

Italy's long coast line means she is well supplied with sea fish while lake and river fish feature in local recipes. Cooking methods are simple, like marinating, then grilling or baking. Generally Italians cook the fish with the head and tail, to keep the flavour, though a big fish like turbot will be cooked in one piece. There are also some wonderful fish soups.

## PIKE

Pike are caught in the mountains of the north and centre. This taper-shaped predator with its ugly mouth is a mass of little bones, embedded in the flesh. For this reason the more sophisticated recipes will serve pike deboned and puréed. In my old recipe the luccio is served whole, leaving the eater with the choice of painstakingly extracting the bones or swallowing them. You might prefer a solid piece of boneless monkfish or tuna!

## RED AND GREY MULLET

The red mullet, triglia, is the most highly-prized fish of the Mediterranean. Apart from its beautiful colour, it can be cooked whole without cleaning. Scrape off the sequin-like scales by drawing a knife from the tail down towards the head.

The grey mullet is called cefalo or muggine. It has a distinctive torpedo-shaped body, with a black back and needs careful cleaning if it was not taken from clean water.

## DORADE

The dorade (or daurade) is a large fish with silvery scales, somewhat similar in taste to the sea bream.

### RASCASSE

The scorfano or scorpion fish is chiefly famous as the fish for broth.

### SARDINES

Pilchards – and a lot of other little fish – go under the name of sarde. These stubby little silver fish, with a blue-green sheen and large papery scales swim in shoals off the south coast and are popularly eaten grilled round all the shores of the Mediterranean.

### EEL

The common eel spends a large part of its life in freshwater and the best come from the lagoon at Comacchio on the east coast. Other eels are fished from the sea and there are many ways of cooking them. The anguilla looks somewhat primitive, but the whitish flesh is delicious roasted or stewed.

Allow for the weight of the head and bony tail when purchasing. Fresh-water eels have fat under the skin at certain times of year, so if they are not already skinned, tie a string round the head under the gills and attach this to a fixed point. Then nick the skin at back of head, get a grip with salted fingers and pull – like ripping sticking plaster. Alternatively, ask your fishmonger!

### ANCHOVY

Anchovies are called acciuga in the north of Italy, and alice round Naples. It is impossible to confuse fresh anchovies with sardines because they are very slender with a sharp nose. Their sides are silvery and the blue-green back turns dark blue or black as more time out of the water elapses. They are best appreciated raw in a vinaigrette marinade.

The canned variety is commonly available, but if you get the chance, try the salted barrel variety – better Italian delicatessens abroad stock these. Prepare barrel anchovies by washing them, then splitting them open to remove the bones from the inside. In Italy anchovies are used as a flavouring for beans and stews.

### DRIED FISH

Dried cod is one of the staples of the Italian peasant. There are two different ways of curing it, one with salt and one without. Both kinds of fish can be used interchangeably, as long as they are soaked first for the appropriate time.

Stoccafisso, stockfish, has been eaten by Italian peasants for 500 years, because it is dried hard and so is absolutely safe in summer temperatures. It is not salted, but is wind-dried, gutted and the head removed, but is otherwise fish-shaped. Other fish than cod are sometimes preserved in this traditional way too.

Baccalà (confusingly, the Venetians use this term for Stoccofisso) are beheaded, split open and salted on ship, then dried on land. They are like thick triangular cardboard sheets, salty and smelling faintly and can be a considerable size. Of the two they are much easier to find in any Mediter-ranean delicatessen.

Stockfish needs to be beaten to break the fibres, and then soaked – usually for 3 days. Salt cod needs 24 hours soaking – done in a bowl in a sink under a running tap to avoid any smell. Thick pieces from the centre of the fish are often fried, thinner trimm-ings flavour stews with tomatoes and other vegetables. Judge the soaking time by the rest of the recipe. The fish must be very moist if there is no further stewing. Lucky Italians can buy these fish ready-prepared!

## SHELLFISH

The main rule for clams and mussels is to discard open ones before you start and closed ones after cooking

### SQUID AND OCTOPUS

The torpedo-shaped squid, with two fins at the end opposite the tentacles are called calamari. Cuttlefish, seppie, are flatter with a frilly fin all round and two of the tentacles are much longer with 'spoons' on the end. Big ones may be stuffed, others cut into strips and fried, and tiny ones served whole.

The preparation is very similar. Pull up the tentacles to turn out the con-tents of the sac (being careful not to puncture the ink bag, which is kept in some recipes). Cut off the tentacles above the eyes and discard everything else. Flex the body slightly to dislodge the transparent cartilage of a squid. Large cuttlefish must be slit down the side to remove the white cuttle bone. Rub off the dark skin with salted hands.

Remove the eyes and beak of an octopus, polpo, and clean inside. For bigger ones you will need to make a slit up to the head and peel the skin off the tentacles, with the rings in the suckers. After this give them a good thumping, like tenderizing a steak.

### SCAMPI

Big ones have enormous claws and it's worth exploring the head and the claws for their edible insides. The back shell is firmer than a prawn's, with spiky edges, and the stomach is pro-tected. To snap the stomach shell, squeeze the two sides together, then peel the legs up and over the back – like taking off a saddle. Nip the tail fin with one hand to release suction and pull the body out with the other hand.

# VEGETABLES

The delights of the Italian vegetable garden are basic to Italian cooking. Vegetables which are well known elsewhere have their particular uses in Italian dishes. For example, celery and carrots are a standard soup flavouring and are used in soffritto (see Bacon).

Some vegetables are particularly identified with the south; aubergines, melanzane, have been eaten there for 900 years. It's important to remove their bitter juices by salting, washing and draining. They otherwise absorb huge amounts of oil during cooking.

Peppers, peperoni, which give such colour, grow to a huge size in the south, where they are grilled or stuffed. The chilli, peperoncini, is also an identifiably southern flavouring.

## CHARD AND BITTER LEAVES

Coste, often known as Swiss chard, is popular round the Mediterranean and becoming better known elsewhere. Fashion has gone in a complete circle and now it is grown for the thick red stems, which have a flavour faintly reminiscent of asparagus, rather than the fleshy dark leaves, which have been used for so long. Chard combines well with pine nuts.

Spinach, spinaci, is not a long-established Italian vegetable, but it has been enthusiastically embraced, and can be substituted for chard, as can the leafy tops of beetroots and turnips.

## CHICORY AND ENDIVE

Chicory and endive are closely related and part of the large family that includes the red radicchio.

Cultivated chicory does not appear in traditional Italian cookery. It is grown in the dark with the leaves tied up tightly to tame it into the familiar white torpedo shape. Wild chicory is a traditional peasant food and slightly bitter to the taste. Its nearest equivalent is curly endive, which can be soaked briefly first to get rid of some of the bitterness.

## ROCKET

Arugula is a peppery salad vegetable. It is a common ingredient in salad leaf mixtures in Italian markets, added to other leaves to make them more interesting. Usually several varieties are on sale. Young spinach is more bitter and less pungent but will do as a substitute.

## COURGETTES AND THEIR FLOWERS

These tiny marrows, less than 15 cm (6 in) long, can be green or yellow and are very popular in Italy. Their Italian name zucchini travelled with them to America, although the British use the French name.

The orange flowers are a delicacy deep-fried or in omelettes. They also look very attractive and are very popular with many chefs outside Italy. Soak them in water with lemon juice for 30 minutes before hulling.

## GLOBE ARTICHOKE

Italians delight in beautiful forms and the handsome carciofi are the huge buds of a type of thistle. They flourish in the limestone soils of south Italy, where they grow at great speed, which gives them the best flavour. There are two main types, one with a pointed head and prickly leaves and one with a rounded head and no prickles.

In the south they are not eaten leaf by leaf as they are further north. Everything served can always be eaten, so they are always cleaned first of inedible parts. Small ones, with soft chokes, are cooked whole, while the bases of larger ones are prepared and served in other dishes. The texture and taste of the tuber Jerusalem artichokes makes an acceptable substitute.

## FENNEL

The most Italian of vegetables, finocchio is sometimes called Florence fennel outside Italy, to distinguish it from the herb of the same name. Its overlapping stems look almost like a bulb and its feathery green tops are saved and are used like a herb, for sprinkling. The sweetness of the vegetable is demonstrated by the old Italian custom of putting fennel on the table, like a fruit, at the end of a meal. It is equally good raw in salads and cooked.

## CELERIAC

In Italy this is called sedano rapa, which means a grating celery, and the root is similar in taste to celery, though it is not really a traditional Italian vegetable. The sweet flavour is strongest in the young roots weighing under 500 g (1 lb). Prepare it like a turnip, which can be used as a substitute. (Of the two, turnip has a tougher skin with more waste). Keep the leaves of celeriac, if you can get them – they make a lovely additional seasoning to the dish.

## SCORZONERA

This thin black root, like a carrot but twice as long, belongs to the dandelion family. The Italian name is used worldwide, since it was bred in Italy. Salsify is very similar to it, though unrelated, and makes a good substitute.

The flavour is sweet and some say oyster-like. To prepare it, remove the base of the roots and leafy tops, brush off the soil and peel or scrape off the skin. It is then cut into 5–10 cm (2–4 inch) lengths. Keep it in water made acid with a little lemon juice until cooked; it is ready when slightly softened.

## ONIONS AND GARLIC

Indispensable as a flavouring for other vegetables, the cipolla is also eaten in its own right: roast, stuffed and in salads. There are several different varieties serving different purposes, the mildest coming from Piedmont. Red ones are used for salads and for their colour in dishes like Fitascetta.

It would be impossible to imagine the Italian kitchen without aglio, garlic. Garlic is frequently fried first in cooking oil to flavour it. Finely chopped and fried with onion in pork fat, it makes a basic kitchen preparation – battuto – which is used as a base for many dishes.

## TOMATOES

The pomodoro, or 'golden apple' has been at the centre of southern Italian cooking since the 18th century, while Naples invented the tomato sauce.

Really ripe tomatoes have few seeds and the skin peels off easily. A few seconds in boiling water may be necessary for less perfect northern specimens. In Italy plum tomatoes are invariably used for cooking, round ones are preferred for salads.

For more than a hundred years the south has canned tomatoes for export. A more recent export, now widely available, is the processed version, passata. The name means sieved, and it is nothing more than tomato pulp, conveniently without skin or pips, unlike tomato paste, which is highly concentrated.

## CEPS

Ceps, porcini in Italy, are the best-flavoured mushrooms of the boletus family. The cap of the fresh mushroom looks like a brown sugar-glazed bun, with a fat stalk.

The flavour of the mushroom is enhanced and intensified by drying, so although it is quite expensive, 30 g (1 oz) is usually enough for a dish. Soak dried porcini for about 20 minutes in warm water, then drain and slice. Add them towards the end of cooking time, so that they do not lose their flavour.

## TRUFFLES

Tartufi are the kings of the edible fungi. Italy has two of the very best. The black truffle grows most profusely round Norcia and Spoleto in Umbria, where pigs are still trained to identify where they are hidden underground. They are in season for Christmas – found from October to December, and are the same truffle that is found in Périgord in France. A truffle looks somewhat like a dirty potato. Cooking brings out its flavour. The so called white truffle – in reality a beige-brown – comes from round the town of Alba. The finest in the world, it is shaved raw over hot food.

Black truffles are sold vacuum-packed with a little liquid in jars, while even the peelings are canned. Once a wild food, available to all finders, the smell of truffle is so pervasive that it affects all food it contacts. Hence the appeal of the truffle or truffle-and-mushroom pastes, and even truffle-flavoured oil.

## HERBS

Some familiar herbs are indispensable to Italian dishes: thyme with everything, rosemary for roasts and barbecues, wild fennel for fish and sausages, the bayleaf as a partner for fish and meat and sage as almost obligatory in the north for pork and beans. Mint is used in combinations that would not be imagined elsewhere, while flat parsley has more flavour than the curly one.

## OREGANO

Luckily for everyone, this is one of the few herbs that taste better dried. Drying accentuates its flavour. Oregano from the south is most pungent and is partnered with a wide range of foods.

## BASIL

A sun-lover, basilico is the perfect partner for tomatoes. But in Liguria it is cultivated for pesto sauce, combined with Parmesan and pine nuts.

## PREBOGGION

A mixed handful of wild herbs, sold in the markets of Genoa, which combine for one mass of flavour. Picking a bunch of wild herbs with as many varieties as possible is a common practice which need not be limited to Italy. They are used to flavour salads and stuffings alike.

## CAPERS

Capers, capperi, are the tight buds of a Mediterranean shrub. They are preserved in sea salt and often in wine vinegar. They have a sharp taste somehow redolent of their dark green colour and provide a good foil to olive oil and rich meats and sauces.

# SOUPS

*There are few things more wholesome and nourishing than a big bowl of real Italian soup — perfect for the cold winter evenings, rich enough for a main meal in summertime.*

JOTA *left (p 31)*
MINESTRONE CON LA ZUCCA *right ( p 21)*

THERE ARE FEW THINGS MORE WHOLESOME and nourishing than a big bowl of real, honest soup. In terms of the peasant household, where wasting food was rightly considered a cardinal sin, a soup neatly solved the problem of how to make something delicious out of the left-overs. Minestrone translates literally as 'Big Soup', in other words a soup which is an entire meal. It originated in Lombardy, a flat, uninterrupted landscape, whose inhabitants are often fog- and snow-bound – making it a perfect setting for the eating of soup. Lombard farms tend to be enormous buildings with plenty of space for families and animals, fortresses against the inclement weather and unsympathetic intruders. Imagine, if you can, being trapped inside your vast farm in mid-winter. There is a huge fire roaring in the grate, and outside all is grey, dark and damp. This is most certainly not the moment for a cheese soufflé with prawn sauce: what you need is a bowl of soup filled with vegetables and rice or pasta, all simmered in the best-quality broth. Into the broth and/or Minestrone itself go any scrap leftovers – to be instantly transformed into something memorable!

In the recipes which come from further south you will discover a certain difference: although the soups are still nourishing and filling, they are considerably less rich and a great deal lighter. This is due principally to the difference in climate – the temperature of a Calabrian winter is somewhat milder than the winter in Friuli, unless you venture high up on the mountains, and even then you won't have the Alpine conditions of the northern areas. In the south, chilli peppers are very popular for keeping you warm – an innocent looking vegetable soup eaten in the Abruzzi villages could have you reaching for the water jug before you can swallow!

The soup recipes which use bread (as opposed to rice, beans and pulses, pasta or potatoes) as their starch base, do so purely for reasons of economy and when you read them they may sound a bit tasteless. But the quality of the bread is the key – bread which is full of flavour and texture will be an admirable base for anything. When making these soups, try to get hold of bread which tastes like bread ought to taste – the home-made variety being the very best!

Tortellini in Brodo – tortellini in a broth – is a very delicate and sophisticated way of serving pasta. The broth should be of the best quality, and it is most important that you seal the little pasta parcels very securely before boiling – if you don't they will almost certainly part company with their filling during cooking! They should be plunged into the broth for literally the very last minutes. It is customary to offer a garnish of grated Parmesan or pecorino cheese when serving soup, and also a little jug of olive oil to dribble over the soup before eating – this enhances the flavour and helps to cool the soup down.

As with all the recipes in this book, I very much hope that these soups will become close friends of yours, and therefore you must feel free to vary the recipes as you use them. After all, in their original settings they would have altered a great deal from one household to another depending on the availability of ingredients and that great unquantifiable, personal taste.

# MINESTRONE ALLA LOMBARDA

## LOMBARD MINESTRONE

This is the original 'big soup' – so stiff it is almost solid cold – containing lots of fresh vegetables, rice and Parmesan cheese to nourish and satisfy.

### SERVES 6

2 sticks celery, very finely chopped
2 carrots, scraped and very finely chopped
2 courgettes, finely sliced
3 floury potatoes, peeled and left whole
450 g (1 lb) ripe tomatoes
50 g (2 oz) pork dripping
a handful of fresh parsley, washed and very finely chopped
1 large clove garlic, peeled and very finely chopped
1 large red onion, finely chopped
2 leaves fresh sage
50 g (1¾ oz) streaky green bacon, finely chopped
2 strips pork belly, cut into fine cubes
8 fresh basil leaves
225 g (8 oz) fresh borlotti beans (or 115 g (4 oz) dried – soaked overnight and brought back to the boil twice)
225 g (8 oz) shelled peas (frozen, only if you really have no alternative)
¼ cabbage, leaves coarsely chopped
½ teaspoon tomato paste
200 g (7 oz) rice or small size pasta
salt and pepper
freshly grated Parmesan cheese
olive oil

Prepare and mix the celery, carrots, courgettes and potatoes. Dip the tomatoes in boiling water. Scoop them out with a slotted spoon, discarding the seeds, quickly peel, then chop them.

Put the dripping, parsley and garlic in a 3 litre (6½ pint) soup pot and mix well. Add the chopped onion, sage leaves, bacon and pork belly. Fry together very carefully until the onion is mushy and transparent, add all the prepared vegetables, except the peas and cabbage, then the basil, beans and tomato paste.

Pour in 3 litres (5 pints) cold water, cover and simmer for 3 hours, stirring occasionally. If at the end of this time the potatoes have not disintegrated into tiny bits, mash them in with a fork to thicken the soup.

If using shelled peas, add them to the soup. After 15 minutes, add the cabbage leaves. Simmer for 15 minutes, then add the rice or pasta, with the frozen peas, if using. Cook rice for 20 minutes or pasta according to the manufacturers' instructions. Stir and taste and adjust the seasoning.

Serve hot in the winter time with olive oil to drizzle over the surface and Parmesan cheese in a bowl to sprinkle on to taste. In the summertime the soup is eaten cold, but not chilled. If wished, let the soup set in individual bowls overnight, then turn it out on to plates, but always serve it with olive oil and Parmesan cheese.

# MINESTRONE CON LA ZUCCA

## MINESTRONE WITH PUMPKIN

This soup always makes a good impression, it's so bright and warming and really does taste as good as it looks! Serve it with a fairly smooth white wine, such as Franciacorta Pinot, which is a good all round soup wine. It is also an excellent accompaniment with egg and cheese dishes and lake or river fish.

### SERVES 4

800 g (1¾ lb) yellow pumpkin, peeled and seeded
salt and pepper
500 ml (18 fl oz) good stock
500 ml (18 fl oz) milk
60 g (2 oz) spaghetti, broken into small pieces
30 g (1 oz) unsalted butter
85 g (3 oz) freshly grated Parmesan cheese

Cut the pumpkin into chunks. Bring a large saucepan of salted water to the boil, add the pumpkin and cook until tender. Drain and mash to a purée. Return to the pan, pour in the stock and milk and stir.

Bring back to the boil, stir in the pasta and cook until tender. Taste and season. Remove the pan from the heat, stir in the butter and Parmesan cheese. Serve very hot.

## ZUPPA DI FINOCCHI

### FENNEL SOUP

This is the perfect soup to eat after several heavy meals as the fennel has marvellous digestive properties. So if you have got to the point where you really can't face anything rich, but want to eat something which is soothing and original, try this easy soup.

SERVES 4—6

*5 large, crunchy fennel bulbs*
*3 large cloves garlic, finely chopped*
*a handful of fresh parsley, finely chopped*
*60 ml (2 fl oz) olive oil*
*salt and pepper*
*4 slices stale white bread*

OX-DRAWN CART *The huge white oxen draw home the forage — an evening scene unaltered in centuries of farming.*

Remove the outer parts of the fennel bulbs and slice the tender white interior into fine, neat strips. Put into a pan with the garlic, parsley, oil and a pinch of salt. Fry gently for about 6 minutes, stirring and turning.

Cover with 1.2 litres (2 pints) cold water or chicken stock if you want a soup with a less gentle flavour. Bring to the boil, then reduce the heat and simmer slowly until the fennel is falling to pieces. Taste and season very generously. Meanwhile, toast the bread in the oven.

Place the toast in the bottom of the soup tureen. Pour the soup over it and serve at once.

# MINESTRA DI RISO, LATTE E CASTAGNE

## CHESTNUT, MILK AND RICE SOUP

Most people either love or hate chestnuts, so perhaps this isn't the best choice for a dinner party or supper where you don't know your guests' tastes too well. If you are a chestnut person, like me, you will love this delicious and very nourishing soup. Its consistency is not unlike creamy porridge – or even rice pudding.

### SERVES 4

*200 g (7 oz) fresh chestnuts*
*salt*
*150 g (5 oz) pudding rice*
*500 ml (18 fl oz) milk*
*30 g (1 oz) unsalted butter*

Pierce the chestnuts with a fork, put them in a pan, cover with lukewarm water, and boil for 5–8 minutes. Drain, then remove the shell and the soft inner skin. Place in a large pan with about 1½ litres (2¾ pints) salted water and boil over a medium heat for 2½ hours until the nuts are disintegrating and the liquid halved.

Add the rice and cook for about 12 minutes, until the rice is half cooked, then add the milk and butter. Cook until the soup is very thick and creamy then season and serve piping hot.

# ACQUACOTTA

## EGG, TOMATO AND MUSHROOM SOUP

Literally meaning 'cooked water', this is an ancient recipe from Tuscany consisting of mushrooms cooked with garlic, oil and tomatoes – the resulting mixture is diluted to soup texture and poured into each plate or soup bowl where slices of coarse toasted bread have been laid to absorb excess liquid. The soup is finished off with grated cheese and eggs to make it more nourishing. Don't be put off by the name: the flavour is delicate, but truly delicious, as ceps are the most flavourful of all mushrooms.

### SERVES 4

*450 g (1 lb) fresh ceps (or other wild mushrooms)*
*4 tablespoons olive oil*
*2 cloves garlic, slightly crushed*
*salt and pepper*
*200 g (7 oz) fresh ripe tomatoes, or equivalent canned,*
*peeled and seeded*
*8 small slices stale white bread*
*3 eggs*
*2 heaped tablespoons freshly grated Parmesan cheese*

Clean the mushrooms, trim and wash them carefully. Dry them thoroughly, then slice. Heat the olive oil in a wide, deep saucepan, capacity about 2 litres (3½ pints). Add the garlic and fry until golden, then add the mushrooms.

Season with salt and pepper and cook for about 15 minutes, then add the tomatoes. Stir in 1 litre (1¾ pints) salted boiling water, cover and simmer until the mushrooms are completely soft, about 10 minutes.

Meanwhile, toast the bread in the oven until crisp. Place 2 slices in the bottom of each soup plate. Beat the eggs with the Parmesan cheese in a soup tureen and as soon as the soup is ready, pour it over the eggs and cheese. Beat again to scramble the eggs, then ladle it into the soup plates over the bread.

TUSCAN FARMSTEAD *The remote Tuscan hills are sparsely dotted with farmsteads like this one, nestling in the borders of a dark wood.*

# MINESTRONE ALLA LIGURE

## LIGURIAN MINESTRONE

This is the Ligurian version of minestrone with lots of fresh herbs and the final addition of a flavourful rosemary pesto stirred into the finished soup.

### SERVES 6

*60 g (2 oz) dried cannellini beans, soaked overnight and brought back to the boil twice*
*olive oil*
*1 large white onion, finely chopped*
*3 sticks celery, finely chopped*
*1 large slice prosciutto crudo, cut into thin strips*
*1 small cabbage – white is best for colour – finely shredded*
*2 large carrots, scraped and finely chopped*
*6 large spinach leaves, trimmed and washed*
*6 large dark green lettuce leaves, washed and chopped*
*1 large tablespoon tomato paste*
*1.2 litres (2 pints) good chicken or vegetable stock*
*1 large clove garlic*
*a handful of fresh parsley*
*2 small sprigs fresh rosemary*
*2 heaped tablespoons freshly grated Parmesan cheese, plus extra for serving*
*¼ dried red chilli pepper*
*200 g (8 oz) pasta, preferably lasagnette or tagliatelle broken into 7.5 cm (3 inch) lengths*

Put 3 tablespoons olive oil in a large pan, capacity 1.5 litres (3 pints). Add the onion, celery and prosciutto and fry gently until the onion is transparent.

Add the beans, cabbage, carrots, spinach, lettuce and tomato paste. Stir and sweat these gently while heating the stock. Pour in the stock and stir. Cover and simmer for about 1½ hours, adding more stock if it seems needed to cover the vegetables well.

Meanwhile, put garlic, parsley, rosemary, Parmesan and chilli into a mortar and pound to a paste. Push this pesto mixture through a sieve and set aside. (Alternatively, use a food processor, then sieve.)

Toss the pasta into the soup and cook until tender, then stir in the pesto mixture. Stir and allow to stand for a few minutes. Ladle out into bowls, cover with grated cheese and serve immediately.

# TORTELLINI IN BRODO

## TORTELLINI IN A BROTH

This is the most classic of all the soups from Emilia Romagna: the rich chicken stock has delicate hand-made pasta parcels filled with minced meat floating on the surface. Making tortellini is an art; on your first practice run you might do better to use a 2-egg quantity of pasta and half the filling.

### SERVES 6

CHICKEN STOCK
*½ a chicken*
*450 g (1 lb) shin of beef*
*1 large carrot, scraped*
*1 onion*
*2 sticks celery, trimmed*
*a handful of fresh parsley*
*2 small cabbage leaves*
*salt and pepper*
PASTA
*300 g (10 oz) plain white flour*
*3 large eggs*
FILLING
*100 g (3½ oz) rump steak, cut into cubes*
*50 g (1¾ oz) turkey breast, cut into cubes*
*30 g (1 oz) butter*
*100 g (3½ oz) mortadella*
*100 g (3½ oz) prosciutto crudo*
*2 eggs*
*a pinch of grated nutmeg*
*200 g (7 oz) freshly grated Parmesan cheese*

To make the broth, put all the ingredients in the bottom of a stock pot, seasoning to taste with salt and pepper. Cover with about 3 litres (5 pints) cold water and bring to the boil. Cover and simmer for about 3 hours. Check seasoning, strain twice and leave to cool overnight.

The next day, make the pasta. Put the flour on to the table in a mound, make a hollow in the centre with your fist. Break the eggs into the hollow. Keeping your fingers stiff, mix the eggs into the flour, then knead together.

Work the dough thoroughly for 15–20 minutes. It should be quite stiff, but golden yellow, elastic and smooth. Cover with a damp clean cloth and leave to rest.

Meanwhile, make the filling. Cook the steak and turkey together in the butter over a gentle heat for 10 minutes. Cool, then mince twice with the mortadella and prosciutto. Mix in the eggs, nutmeg, salt and pepper and 150 g (5 oz) of the cheese. Set aside.

Roll out the pasta as thinly as possible, fold it in half and roll it again. Continue in this way until it snaps at the fold as you roll it. When you hear the snap it is ready to use. Roll it out again very thinly and cut it into 4 cm (1½ inch) circles with a pastry cutter or upturned wine glass.

Place a tiny mound of filling in the centre of each circle, fold in half and press the edges together tightly to prevent the filling escaping during cooking. When they are all folded securely, shape into crescents. Take each one and twist it around your index finger, secure the ends together tightly (use a dab of cold water if you like) and slide the completed tortellini off the end of your finger. Lay them out in neat rows on floured tea cloths, without overlapping. There may be filling left over – it depends on how good you become at rolling the pasta thinly.

Bring the broth to the boil. Slide the tortellini in and cook for 2–3 minutes. Serve at once with the remaining cheese sprinkled on top. I always drink a generous bottle of Lambrusco with this dish.

COMMUNAL SUPPER *The older generation get together for a special evening meal al fresco, accompanied by plenty of good local wine.*

# ZUPPA DI ZUCCHINE

## COURGETTE SOUP

This summer soup of courgettes, fresh basil, eggs, olive oil, bread and cheese is a speciality of the southern province of Naples. Here the black soil along the coast supports a profusion of vegetables. Very fresh courgettes, with glossy skins, are crucial – and also young tender ones. Their maximum size should be 15 cm (6 inches) long by 4 cm (1½ inches) diameter and when they are cut the seeds should be small. The quality of the vegetables will make the difference between a good soup and a tasteless one.

SERVES 4

*5 very fresh courgettes, washed and trimmed*
*3 tablespoons olive oil*
*salt and pepper*
*2 eggs*
*3 heaped tablespoons freshly grated Parmesan cheese*
*50 g (1¾ oz) fresh parsley, finely chopped*
*8 fresh basil leaves, finely chopped*
*8 slices stale white bread*

Cut the unpeeled courgettes into neat small squares. Heat the oil in a saucepan, add the courgettes and fry gently together, turning frequently, for about 2 minutes.

Pour 1.2 litres (2 pints) cold water (or stock) over the courgettes, season with salt and pepper and stir well. Cover, bring to the boil, then simmer for 45 minutes.

Beat the eggs in a bowl with the cheese and the herbs. Pour into the hot soup, beat through to scramble the eggs and set aside off the heat. Toast the bread and lay 2 slices in each soup bowl. Ladle the slightly cooled soup over the bread and serve.

# PANCOTTO
# CON RUCOLA E PATATE

## ROCKET AND POTATO SOUP

This recipe from Apulia dates back to the Daunian civilisation 2,500 years ago. It's one of the simplest soups, but bursting with flavour and with a lovely texture – and the rocket is said to purify the blood.

### SERVES 4

*450 g (1 lb) potatoes, peeled and thickly sliced*
*450 g (1 lb) rocket (or trimmed spinach)*
*salt*
*8 slices stale white bread*
*100 ml (3¼ fl oz) olive oil*
*1 dried red chilli*
*2 cloves garlic, sliced into thin strips*

Cover the potatoes with about 1.5 litres (2½ pints) cold water. Bring to the boil and cook for 10 minutes. Meanwhile, wash and trim the rocket.

Add the rocket to the potatoes (coarsely chopped if you like, although it isn't traditional to do so!). Spinach doesn't have quite the same pungent taste as rocket, but it nevertheless makes a popular soup. Continue to cook the soup, stirring occasionally, until the potatoes are mushy. Season with salt and pepper, then add the bread. Stir the soup and pour it into a soup tureen.

Heat the oil in a pan, add the garlic and the chilli and fry for about 8 minutes, then discard the chilli. Pour the oil and garlic over the soup, stir through and serve at once.

FRESHLY BAKED LOAVES *Straight from an old-fashioned, wood-burning oven, the hot loaves are set to cool off on a cloth.*

# PANE COTTO CON ALLORO

## BREAD AND CHEESE SOUP

This soup crops up all over the country in various forms and has its roots in times of poverty when nothing was ever wasted, not even the leftover stale bread. It is a nourishing soup which can be thrown together quickly, though somewhat spartan for modern tastes. You might prefer to start with stock.

### SERVES 4

*salt*
*2 fresh bay leaves or 1 dried bay leaf*
*75 ml (2½ fl oz) olive oil*
*8 stale white bread rolls, broken into smallish pieces*
*8 tablespoons freshly grated pecorino cheese*

Bring 1.2 litres (2 pints) water to the boil with a pinch of salt. Add the bay leaves or leaf and the oil. Stir and simmer for about 5 minutes. Throw in the bread and stir. Pour out into a soup tureen and sprinkle the cheese over the top.

# JOTA

## HEARTY WINTER SOUP

This is the perfect sort of soup to eat on really cold winter days. I like to prepare it in time to serve upon return from a trek in the forest through the snow. Nothing else is necessary after a couple of bowlfuls, except maybe a dish of baked apples or some sliced oranges. A good rich red wine like a Merlot complements the flavours perfectly.

### SERVES 6

*300 g (10 oz) dried borlotti, kidney or cannellini beans,*
*soaked overnight*
*150 g (5 oz) pork belly, diced*
*2 tablespoons vegetable oil or pork dripping*
*1 tablespoon plain flour*
*50 g (1¾ oz) lard*
*1 large onion, very finely chopped*
*½ teaspoon dried sage*
*2 cloves garlic, very finely chopped*
*a handful of fresh parsley, very finely chopped*
*5 tablespoons polenta (yellow cornmeal)*
*100 g (3½ oz) smoked streaky bacon or pancetta*
*300 g (10 oz) sauerkraut*
*salt*

Drain the beans, put them in a pan, cover with water and bring to the boil. After 10 minutes, drain and rinse, then cover with about 1.5 litres (2½ pints) cold water and the diced pork belly. Bring to the boil, cover and simmer slowly. Fry the oil and flour together to make a roux, then stir it into the beans. Continue to cook for approximately half-an-hour.

Fry the lard, onion, sage, garlic and parsley together until amalgamated. Add the polenta then add this to the beans. Stir and simmer for another 30 minutes. Fry the bacon until the fat is running and sizzling, add the sauerkraut and stir together, then mix into the soup. Taste for seasoning.

# ZUPPA DI FAGIOLI

## BEAN SOUP

The secret of success is in using fresh beans. If you really cannot get hold of any, the dried variety will have to do, but the flavour won't be quite the same. Always bring the beans to a full boil after soaking them. Wash and drain them, then use as fresh. The soup does not necessarily contain onion but it is needed for flavouring dried beans.

SERVES 4

650 g (1½ lb) fresh borlotti beans or 300 g (10 oz) dried, soaked overnight and drained
1 large onion, finely chopped
1 large stick celery, finely chopped
50 g (1¾ oz) fresh parsley, finely chopped
about 50 ml (1¾ fl oz) olive oil
30 g (1 oz) bacon or ham fat (preferably smoked), finely chopped, or 115 g (4 oz) pork belly, chopped
2 tablespoons tomato paste
salt and pepper

Cover the fresh or soaked beans in cold water, bring to the boil and simmer gently until soft. Dried beans will take about an hour. Mix the parsley, celery and bacon or ham fat together very thoroughly to make a paste.

Heat the olive oil and fat in a deep pan, add the onion, celery and parsley mixture (and the pork belly, if using) and fry together, until the onion is soft. Add the tomato paste and mix together, adding about 6 tablespoons of warm water to dilute the purée.

Drain the cooked beans, add to the pan and stir. Pour in enough boiling water to make the quantity of soup you require – about 1 litre (1¾ pints). Add the water slowly and carefully so that you have just the right amount and don't finish up with a watery mess. Toast the bread in the oven and place in the bottom of the soup tureen. Cook the soup, covered, for 10 minutes then pour over the bread and serve.

# LA MES – CIUA

## MIXED PULSE SOUP

This very different soup is included for historical reasons. The original version contained only dried maize, chick peas and beans, flavoured with cheese – I have used fresh corn and added some flavouring ingredients. It is a speciality of La Spezia and the surrounding area – born out of a time when there was not enough flour to make bread, nor enough beans or dried maize to make a dish, and certainly no meat available to simply waste in a soup.

### SERVES 6

*300 g (10 oz) dried chick peas*
*300 g (10 oz) dried cannellini beans or*
*white butter beans*
*1 teaspoon bicarbonate of soda*
*kernels from 3 corn cobs*
*salt and freshly ground black pepper*

SACKFULS OF BEANS *The best and cheapest way of buying dried pulses in Italy is straight from the sack.*

*1.2 litres (2 pints) stock*
*1 onion, finely chopped*
*4 cloves garlic, crushed*
*4 tablespoons tomato paste*
*freshly grated Parmesan cheese*

Sort through the pulses, removing bad ones. Put the chick peas in a large bowl, add a pinch of bicarbonate and cover with water. Soak the beans in a different bowl the same way and leave overnight. Also check the packet instructions – modern varieties of chick pea cook faster than beans; with others the reverse is true.

The next day, drain the beans, wash, put in a large pan and cover with more water. Boil quickly for 10 minutes. Drain and put them in a large pan with the onion, garlic, tomato paste, stock and a pinch of salt, and bring to the boil. Drain and wash the chick peas and put in a separate pan. Add salt and water and bring to the boil. After 10 minutes, add the corn kernels to the chick peas. Cook for about 30 minutes until the beans are mushy and the chick peas and corn are soft.

Pour the chick pea mixture into the beans with some of their liquid – you should have about 1.75 litres (3 pints). Season and cook gently for a further 15 minutes. Each person should add freshly ground pepper and Parmesan cheese to taste.

# CIPOLLATA

## ONION AND TOMATO SOUP

This very simple tomato-flavoured onion soup from Umbria is scented with fresh basil and enriched with golden-green olive oil. If you are using fresh tomatoes with a poor colour, add a tablespoon of tomato paste.

### SERVES 4

*1 kg (2¼ lb) large golden onions, thinly sliced*
*50 g (1¾ oz) ham fat, diced*
*1 tablespoon olive oil*
*7 fresh basil leaves*
*salt and pepper*
*400 g (14 oz) soft, fresh ripe tomatoes, sieved, or passata*
*freshly grated Parmesan cheese*
*2 eggs, beaten*

Cover the sliced onions with cold water and leave to soak overnight.

The next day, drain the onions. Fry the ham fat and olive oil together for 5 minutes then add the onions and basil and season with salt and pepper. Stir well, then cover and leave to sweat slowly until the onions have softened but are not coloured.

Stir in the sieved tomatoes and 1 litre (1¾ pints) water. Cover and simmer for a further 1½ hours. Remove from the heat, cover with Parmesan cheese and quickly beat in the eggs. Serve as a thick and very substantial soup with toasted bread or bruschetta – bread grilled with oil and garlic – and plenty of robust red wine. Colli del Trasimeno is a good choice.

# FAVATA

## PORK AND BEAN SOUP

This is one of those thick, full-of-goodness, nourishing soups which relies on plenty of time in order for it to come out right – don't skimp, even if you leave it bubbling for a whole day or night you will only be making it even tastier. Add the oil just before you serve as it should not cook, but should cool and flavour the soup.

### SERVES 6

*400 g (14 oz) dried broad beans*
*400 g (14 oz) small pork chops*
*300 g (10 oz) Italian pork sausages*
*300 g (10 oz) pork belly*
*olive oil*
*a large pinch of mixed dried herbs*
*2 fresh tomatoes, peeled and chopped*
*1 stick celery, chopped*
*1 onion, chopped*
*1 carrot, chopped*
*¼ small cabbage, shredded*
*¼ fennel bulb, chopped*
*3 cloves garlic, crushed*

Soak the beans overnight, then wash them. Put in a large pan, cover with water and boil rapidly for 5 minutes. Drain and wash them, then cut each one through the skin, making a slit in each bean on one side only. Set aside.

Cut all the meats into small chunks and put in a deep flameproof casserole with a little olive oil. Fry gently together until slightly browned, then add the herbs, tomatoes, celery, onion and carrot. Pour over 3 litres (5 pints) of water and bring to a slow, steady simmer.

When the vegetables are fairly tender, add the broad beans and all the remaining vegetables. Stir well, then cover and cook for another 2½ hours at a slow simmer. Remove from the heat, stir in 2 tablespoons olive oil and serve with plenty of coarse country-style bread.

FAVATA

# PASTA, PIZZA, RICE, POLENTA

*Home-made pastas, delicately stuffed, delight the eye and the palate; pizza and polenta provide hearty, rib-sticking nourishment; and the humble rice grain provides the key to some magnificent risottos.*

TORTA RUSTICA *left (p 46)* STRANGOLAPRIEVE *right (p 40)*

A PLATE OF PIPING HOT PASTA dressed with a rich, brightly-coloured sauce is one of the most satisfying dishes I can think of. And surely nothing is more rib-sticking and warming in the winter than a slab of polenta surmounted by a gloriously rich stew. In summertime, savoury pies, cakes and pizza make mouthwatering companions for lunching al fresco. Then there is rice, that self-effacing, humble-looking grain which happens to be the key to some magnificent dishes when combined with the right accompaniments — everything from eel to red wine and beans. For smaller appetites, these dishes will suffice as a meal in themselves, but traditionally they are only one dish in the procession of courses — following an antipasto of cured meats and pickles and preceding a simple dish of meat and vegetables, or fish or cheese and egg dishes.

In almost all cases, the recipes for pasta in this section call for the pasta to be made by hand. This could cause a few problems for beginners, but after just a little practice I can assure you that you will find it very easy. When you first make pasta, the main thing is not to worry too much about what it looks like! Basic rules apply: make it all about the same thickness so that it will cook evenly, and for the same reason, make the separate pieces roughly the same size as each other. Seal pasta parcels with great care so the filling won't escape.

Polenta, or cornmeal, is now widely available and I am quite confident that it will become extremely popular! If you buy polenta which is in a packet, such as Valsugana brand, the cooking procedure will be much faster and easier — so use this kind for any recipe which involves a short cooking or baking time. Loose sold polenta must be cooked very slowly and for a fairly long time, with somebody constantly stirring to prevent disastrous sticking and disgusting lumpiness. You can buy yellow or white polenta, and it is entirely a matter of personal taste which you choose, although the experts say that the white version is better with fish than the yellow.

The eventual texture of the polenta is also very much a personal taste and it may help to imagine that you are making porridge. Some like it runnier, some like it very much thicker, and it does all depend upon what you are serving it with. Polenta on its own is nothing to get excited about, but just try it with slices of gooey, very ripe Gorgonzola, so that the very hot polenta melts the cheese into an amazing, delicious taste experience, and you will never look at bread and cheese again! Leftover polenta is allowed to cool and solidify completely, then is sliced into thickish strips and fried in olive oil until hot and crisp or grilled until charred on the outside.

Once you have made it half a dozen times, you will begin to experiment with accompaniments and different textures until you find your own favourite. As a child, I was always given polenta in a soup plate, covered with warm milk and finished off with a knob of butter — I have yet to taste anything that is quite so good.

# CASUMZIEEI AMPEZZANI

## BEETROOT PASTA POCKETS WITH POPPY SEEDS

This unusual type of ravioli from the Veneto has a filling of beetroot and ricotta cheese and is dressed with poppy seeds, butter and grated cheese.

### SERVES 4

*500 g (1 lb 2 oz) beetroot, boiled in salted water until tender*
*130 g (4½ oz) unsalted butter*
*75 g (2½ oz) ricotta cheese*
*salt*
*4 eggs*
*about 60 g (2 oz) fresh white breadcrumbs*
*400 g (14 oz) plain white flour*
*150 – 175 ml (5 – 6 fl oz) milk*
*4 teaspoons poppy seeds*
*freshly grated Parmesan cheese*

Peel and mash the beetroot to a soft pulp. Melt about half the butter in a saucepan, add the mashed beetroot and stir together. Add the ricotta cheese and mix it in thoroughly. Remove from the heat, tip into a bowl and add 2 eggs, a little salt and enough breadcrumbs to make a fairly thick, tacky mixture.

Make a smooth dough by kneading together the flour, the remaining 2 eggs and as much milk as is needed, for about 10 – 15 minutes. Then roll it out very thinly and cut it into equal-sized circles with a pastry cutter or an upturned wine glass. Put a little of the beetroot filling in the centre of each circle, fold them in half and press them closed firmly with your fingertips.

Bring a very large pan of water to the boil, tip the ravioli in and cook them for 4 – 5 minutes until they float to the surface. Scoop them out with a fish slice or large slotted spoon and place them in a warmed bowl.

Meanwhile, melt the remaining butter in a small pan. Pour the butter over the ravioli, scatter the poppy seeds and Parmesan cheese to taste over them, toss them very gently and serve at once.

# TORTELLI CON PATATE

## PASTA POCKETS WITH A POTATO FILLING

These parcels of very simple hand-made pasta from Emilia Romagna are filled with a potato stuffing.

### SERVES 4

*450 g (1 lb) plain white flour*
*1 egg*
*salt*
*100 g (3½ oz) unsalted butter, cubed*
*100 g (3½ oz) freshly grated Parmesan cheese*
#### FILLING
*800 g (1 lb 12 oz) potatoes, peeled*
*1 large onion, finely chopped*
*4 cloves garlic, finely chopped*
*100 g (3½ oz) streaky bacon or pancetta, finely chopped*
*salt and freshly ground black pepper*
*150 g (5 oz) ricotta cheese or half and half cottage cheese and sheeps' milk Greek yoghurt*
*a pinch of grated nutmeg*
*a handful of freshly grated Parmesan cheese*

To make the filling, boil the potatoes until soft, mash them thoroughly and set aside. Process the onion, garlic and bacon or pancetta together in a food processor until mushy but not puréed, then fry until the fat runs and the onion is soft and transparent.

Stir the mashed potatoes and add plenty of black pepper. Mix in the ricotta or cottage cheese and yoghurt, nutmeg, Parmesan cheese, salt and more pepper. Mix thoroughly and set aside to cool completely.

Put the flour and a pinch of salt on the table in a mound, make a hole in the centre with your fist, break in the egg and add enough water to make a smooth elastic dough. You will have to knead it for about 20 minutes.

When the dough feels elastic and manageable, roll it out as thinly as possible. Cut into rectangles about 4 x 7 cms, (1½ x 2¾ inches). Put a little filling in the centre of each one and fold it in half. Seal the 3 open edges with a fork.

Bring a large saucepan of salted water to the boil, add the pasta and cook for about 4 minutes. Scoop out with a slotted spoon and transfer to a warm bowl. Scatter the butter over the pasta and toss carefully. Sprinkle with Parmesan cheese and serve.

# STRANGOLAPRIEVE

## PRIESTSTRANGLERS

The story behind this delicious dish is that it was reserved for the occasions when the priest came to call. Priests being notoriously either underfed or very greedy, they would tuck into this dish so voraciously that they would virtually choke themselves. There is another story which claims that the idea *was* to choke the priest!

### SERVES 6

*570 g (1¼ lb) plain white flour*
*200 g (7 oz) semolina*
*salt and pepper*
*450 g (1 lb) fresh ripe tomatoes, cut in half*
*a handful of fresh parsley*
*4 sprigs of fresh basil*
*1 large stick celery with leaves, quartered*
*1 large onion, quartered*
*50 g (1¾ oz) unsalted butter*
*freshly grated Parmesan cheese*

Put the flour and semolina on the table top in a mound. Plunge your clenched fist into the mound, then add a pinch of salt and just enough warm water to allow you to begin kneading. (The emphasis here is on elbow grease rather than more liquid!)

Knead, roll and fold until you have a smooth and elastic dough, no softer than average bread dough – if anything somewhat stiffer. It will take 20–30 minutes. Cover the dough with a damp cloth and leave to rest.

Put the tomatoes, parsley, basil, celery, onion, oil and salt and pepper into a saucepan, cover and simmer slowly in their own juices until the tomatoes fall apart. Leave to cool, then, push it through a mouli or sieve into another pan. Stir and keep warm until required.

Roll out the rested dough into sections no larger than your little finger. Cut each section into 5 or 6 pieces, and rock them to and fro on the table to hollow them out slightly, pressing down very hard with your thumb. Bring a large saucepan of salted water to the boil, add the pasta and cook for 2–3 minutes, scooping them out as soon as they return to the surface. Pour over the warm tomato sauce, and add the butter and plenty of Parmesan cheese. Toss it all together and serve at once.

# PANSOTTI AU PREBOGGION CON SALSA DI NOCI

## WILD HERB PASTA POCKETS WITH WALNUT SAUCE

Preboggion is a handful of mixed, wild, edible herbs, widely sold in all the main Genoese markets. Traditionally, preboggion must include wild borage, lovage, dog's tooth, sorrel, wild chicory, wild onion and wild chervil but can also include anything else you come across! To achieve the same effect, use as many fresh garden herbs (and wild ones if possible) as you have available. Both the pasta pockets and the sauce have a wonderful flavour.

### SERVES 4

#### FILLING

*1 kg (2 lb) mixed fresh herbs and very young spinach mixed together*
*150 g (5 oz) ricotta cheese*
*50 g (1¾ oz) freshly grated Parmesan cheese*
*2 eggs, lightly beaten*
*1 clove garlic, finely chopped*
*salt*

#### SAUCE

*450 g (1 lb) unshelled walnuts*
*75 g (2½ oz) stale bread, soaked until mushy in cold water*
*1 clove garlic*
*salt*
*4 tablespoons sour milk*
*4 tablespoons olive oil*
*3 tablespoons unsalted butter*
*8 tablespoons grated Parmesan cheese*

#### PASTA

*400 g (14 oz) plain white flour*
*about 120 ml (4 fl oz) cold water*
*2 teaspoons white wine*

#### TO SERVE

*freshly grated Parmesan cheese*
*butter*

HOME-MADE RAVIOLI *These home-made ravioli look dainty enough to be the handiwork of a seamstress!*

To make the filling, cook the herbs and spinach together in a pan of boiling salted water. Drain and squeeze between your hands, then mince in a blender or food processor to a smooth green goo. Mix in the ricotta and Parmesan cheeses, eggs and garlic. Season to taste with salt.

To make the sauce, crack the nuts, then blanch them in boiling water for 30 seconds to loosen the inner skins. Peel off the skins. Remove the bread from the water and squeeze dry in your fist. Grind the nuts in a blender or herb mill – this produces a finer texture than a food processor – with the garlic and a pinch of salt. (Using a food processor you will need to pound the nuts in a mortar afterwards.) Gradually add the squeezed-out bread with a little sour milk if it is too stiff. Process until smooth, then sieve into a bowl. Stir in the sour milk and the oil (more or less depending upon what consistency you prefer), taste and adjust seasoning. Keep the sauce at room temperature.

To make the pasta, put the flour on the table in a mound. Make a hole in the centre with your fist and pour in the water and wine. Combine the flour with the liquid, knead to a smooth white dough and set aside to rest for a little while under a clean, damp cloth.

Roll out the dough as thinly as possible and cut into triangles measuring about 7.5 cm (3 inches) on each side. Put a tiny amount of filling in the middle of each one, fold over to make a smaller triangle and press tightly closed with your finger tips (they must be well sealed or the filling will fall out during cooking).

Cook the pasta in boiling salted water for about 4 minutes, drain and dress with the sauce, tossing carefully so as not to split them. Serve with grated Parmesan cheese and butter dotted about on top.

41

# CAVATIEDDI CON LA RUCOLA

## TINY PASTA SHELLS WITH ROCKET

Cavatieddi look like small pasta seashells. In this recipe they are cooked with rocket to give them a distinctive flavour, then dressed with a plain tomato sauce. Knead the pasta dough with as much energy and gusto as possible. Both the red, white and green colours and the texture of the dish are most attractive.

### SERVES 4

*100 g (3½ oz) semolina*
*200 g (7 oz) strong white flour*
*tepid salted water*
*1 large onion, finely chopped*
*2 sticks celery, finely chopped*
*1 clove garlic, finely chopped*
*1 carrot, finely chopped*
*2 tablespoons olive oil*
*500 ml (18 fl oz) passata or sieved tomato*
*salt and pepper*
*450 g (1 lb) rocket, washed, or spinach, trimmed*
*freshly grated pecorino cheese, to taste*

Sift the semolina and flour together twice on to the table top. Make them into a mound. Plunge your fist into the centre of the pile, pour in a little tepid salty water. Begin to knead together – you are trying to achieve the same consistency as bread dough, stiffer, but no softer. After about 25 minutes you should have reached the right texture. Cover the dough with a damp tea cloth.

To form the pasta shapes, break off pieces of the dough, keeping the rest covered. Roll each piece into a cylinder about 30–40 cm (12–16 inches) long. Each cylinder should be no thicker than 1 cm (¾ inch) and each piece of dough must be worked quickly to prevent it drying out. When the cylinder of dough is the right length and thickness, cut it into discs with a sharp knife. Then poke the point of the knife into the centre of each disc and roll it up on itself, to make it slightly concave. This used to be done rolling the pasta several times along the wood grain of a rough table top, which also marked the outside. They should look like small seashells.

When all the dough has been rolled and shaped, leave the cavatieddi uncovered to dry in the air overnight. Turn over to dry the underside. When they are completely dried out, they are ready for cooking in water.

The next day, fry the onion, celery, garlic and carrot in the oil until the onion is soft and transparent. Pour in the passata and stir. Season with salt and pepper, cover and leave to simmer for about 30 minutes.

Put the rocket in a saucepan cover with cold water and a pinch of salt and boil briefly until tender. Double the quantity of water, return to the boil and add in the pasta. Cook until al dente (tender but still with some bite).

Drain the pasta and rocket together, transfer to a warmed bowl, pour over the tomato sauce. Toss together thoroughly, scatter pecorino cheese over it all and serve.

An alternative is to dress the cavatieddi quite simply with 115 ml (4 fl oz) of olive oil in which you have fried 3 cloves of garlic and 2 salted anchovies. The oil must be of the very best quality.

# PASTA CON SUGO DI LEPRE

## PASTA WITH HARE SAUCE

In Sardinia, wide use is made of Pasta Asciutta (literally translated as dry pasta, it actually means pasta which is boiled, drained and dressed with a sauce). In the hunting season, the sauces are often made with wild boar, hare or other locally shot game. Traditionally, the blood is an essential part of this dish and the ideal would be to use a freshly shot animal which you have hung yourself and which you can then skin and gut as you require. However, if you do not want to do it yourself, order a jointed hare or rabbit in advance from your butcher and ask him to keep the blood for you separately.

SERVES 4

75 g (2½ oz) streaky bacon
75 ml (3 fl oz) olive oil
1 small hare or rabbit, divided into 8 joints,
with its blood
2 large onions, thinly sliced
2 large cloves garlic, crushed
1 tablespoon plain flour
1 bottle rich red wine
salt and pepper
a few cloves
a large pinch of cinnamon
a large pinch of dried mixed herbs
bouquet garni
400 g (14 oz) spaghetti
freshly grated pecorino sardo cheese, to taste

Fry the bacon in deep flameproof casserole with the oil, then add the hare and brown it all over. Add the onions and garlic and fry for a few minutes until the onions are golden and soft.

Sprinkle the flour in and cook for 5 minutes, then pour in the wine. Add the salt and pepper to taste, the cloves, cinnamon, dried mixed herbs and bouquet garni. Stir it all together, cover and simmer for about 1½ hours.

Bring a large pan of salted water to the boil, add the spaghetti and cook until al dente (tender but still firm to the bite). Drain and transfer to a warm bowl.

Pour the sauce from the hare over the pasta, toss together thoroughly with as much grated pecorino cheese as you like. Arrange into 4 portions on plates and put 2 pieces of hare on top of each pile of spaghetti. Serve at once. Alternatively, serve the spaghetti with the sauce and serve the hare as as second course with vegetables and potatoes or salad.

Instead of spaghetti, you might like to try a wide ribbon noodle. This is traditional in Tuscany, although it is rather unusual to find a celebrated pasta dish in the northern part of the country. In Pappardelle con la lepre, wide home-made noodles are served with a hare and red wine sauce rather similar to this one.

STRINGS OF RED ONIONS *Strung up high out of the damp, onions can keep for surprisingly long periods. This type of onion makes the colourful topping for* FITASCETTA *(p 48).*

DAWN IN AN OLIVE GROVE *(p 44) The proprietor enjoys the sun rise in his well-tended grove, and is carrying his gun to scare off any marauding birds.*

# LASAGNE INCASSETTATE

## OVEN-BAKED LASAGNE

This most traditional and old-fashioned layered lasagne bake comes from the Marche region of Italy on the Adriatic coast. In other areas, the pasta, sauce and cheeses are served separately so each person can add as much or as little as they like. The cream is a modern addition.

SERVES 4

*300 g (10 oz) plain flour*
*3 eggs*
*1½ tablespoons olive oil*
*salt*

FILLING AND CONDIMENT

*50 g (1¾ oz) fat pancetta or ham fat (preferably smoked)*
*75 g (2½ oz) unsalted butter*
*1 onion, chopped*
*2 fat garlic cloves, finely chopped*
*225 g (8 oz) veal, pork or lamb, finely chopped*
*225 g (8 oz) chicken giblets*
*1 chicken breast, chopped into cubes*
*200 ml (7 fl oz) dry white wine*
*1 chicken liver, cleaned and chopped*
*200 ml (7 fl oz) double cream*
*pinch of dried oregano*
*5 tablespoons finely chopped parsley*
*salt and pepper*
*75 g (2½ oz) Parmesan cheese, freshly grated*
*75 g (2½ oz) Gruyère cheese, grated*
*1 small white truffle (optional)*

Make the pasta, adding the eggs to the flour with salt and just enough oil to make it smooth. Knead very thoroughly for 5 minutes in a food processor, 15–20 minutes by hand.

To make the filling, fry the pancetta or fat in half the butter then add the onion and garlic. After 5 minutes, add the meat and fry for 5 minutes. Add the chicken giblets, chopped breast and breast bone, and wine and cook for 5 minutes. Cover and simmer very slowly for about 1 hour, adding water if necessary.

Roll out the pasta several times, folding it in half and rolling it again each time. Keep doing this until there is an audible snap as you roll the pin over the fold and push the air out. The pasta is then ready: alternatively, use a pasta machine, which rolls and rerolls thinly.

Roll out the dough as thinly as possible; this is important as it puffs slightly when cooked. Then cut it into wide strips (like wide tagliatelle). Bring a large pan of salted water to the boil. Cook the pasta a few strips at a time, until only half cooked (about 3 minutes), drain it, and plunge it into a sink of cold water. If making the lasagne ahead, drain it again and lay it out on tea cloths to dry, making sure the strips don't touch.

To complete the filling, remove the chicken giblets and discard all the bones. Chop the meat and return it to the pan. Add the chicken liver, cream, oregano and parsley, season and cook for 5 more minutes.

To assemble, butter a 1.8-litre (3-pint) dish and arrange a layer of pasta in the bottom with a little sauce and some of each cheese. Continue layer by layer, adding a little butter, until everything is used, spooning the remaining liquid over the top and ending with a layer of cheese. If you are using the truffle, shave it lightly over the finished dish. Dot with any remaining butter. Bake in a moderate oven (180°C, 350°F, gas mark 4) for 20–30 minutes.

# TORTA RUSTICA

## RUSTIC SAVOURY CAKE

Essentially this is a southern Italian savoury pizza cake. It's ideally suited to outdoor events such as wine or oil harvest or fruit picking because the filling is inside the dough. It's prepared for peasant festivities, with a variety of fillings – this is the most classic.

SERVES 6

*400 g (14 oz) plain flour*
*salt and pepper*
*45 ml (1½ fl oz) olive oil plus extra for frying*
*3 tablespoons dry white wine*
*225 g (8 oz) ham, sliced very thick and cubed*
*225 g (8 oz) ricotta cheese*
*1 large or 2 small mozzarella cheeses, cubed*
*150 g (5 oz) caciocavallo cheese, cubed*
*2 eggs, beaten*
*1 tablespoon granulated sugar*

Mix the flour with a pinch of salt, the oil and the wine and just enough water to bind it, about 115 ml (4 fl oz). Knead to a smooth elastic dough, then roll it out thinly.

Oil a cake tin large enough to take the dough and all the other ingredients – a 22 cm (8½ inch) spring-release tin is ideal. Line the tin with two-thirds of the rolled out dough, pressing it up the sides.

Fry the ham in a little oil, remove from the heat and stir in the 3 cheeses. Remove 1 teaspoon of beaten egg and set it aside. Stir the rest of the egg into the ham and cheese, add a little pepper, stir once more and tip into the lined cake tin, smoothing it with a spoon.

Slice the remaining one-third of the dough into wide strips and lay them across the filled cake tin in a tight lattice, covering the filling completely. Press the edges together tightly all the way around. Brush with the reserved spoonful of egg, sprinkle with the sugar and bake in a moderate oven (180°C, 350°F, gas mark 4) for about 45 minutes. Serve either cold or warm at any picnic.

MOTOR TRUCK WITH LEMONS AND CHILLIES *The fruit and chillies still on the branch could not provide a more typically Mediterranean shock of colour.*

# FITASCETTA

## RED ONION PIZZA

Serve this flat, fragrant, savoury cake with a selection of salami and plenty of icy white wine.

SERVES 4

PIZZA
*325 g (11 oz) plain flour*
*a pinch of salt*
*15 g ($\frac{1}{2}$ oz) fresh yeast, diluted in a little warm water, left to froth up in the airing cupboard or warm place*
*450 g (1 lb) red onions, finely sliced and soaked in cold water for about 10 minutes*
*50 g (1$\frac{3}{4}$ oz) unsalted butter*
*salt and pepper*
*olive oil*
*a large sprig of fresh rosemary*
*1 tablespoon light brown sugar or 1 teaspoon coarse salt*

Put all but 3 tablespoons of the flour on to the table top. Make a hollow in the centre with your fist and put the salt and yeast in the hollow. Mix together and knead with as much water as it takes to make a smooth elastic bread dough. Rub the remaining flour over the table top and your hands. When the dough is smooth and well worked, cover it with a cloth and leave in a warm place to double in size – an hour or more.

Drain the onions and fry them in the butter as slowly as you can – until they melt. Season with salt and pepper.

Knead the dough briefly with a little warm water, roll it out like a long sausage, then form it into a circle, keeping the middle hole as large as possible. Oil an ovenproof tray and place the circle on it, flattening it slightly.

Spread the onions all over the dough, making sure they don't drop down into the middle hole! Break the rosemary into pieces and stick them into the dough at even intervals. Scatter the sugar or salt over the top and bake in a moderately hot oven (200°C, 400°F, gas mark 6) for 30 minutes. Eat warm or cold.

# PITTA CHICCULIATA

## CALABRIAN PIZZA

This is a pizza with the filling on the inside. Fillings inside pitta can be all kinds of things, from basil, tomato and olive to sausages and cheese.

### SERVES 4

*450 g (1 lb) plain flour plus extra for kneading*
*a pinch of salt*
*20 g (¾ oz) fresh yeast, diluted in a little warm water,*
*left to froth up in the airing cupboard or warm place*
*1 large clove garlic*
*olive oil*
*1 kg (2¼ lb) fresh ripe tomatoes, peeled, seeded*
*and chopped*
*50 g (1¾ oz) salted anchovies, washed and filleted*
*50 g (1¾ oz) salted capers, washed*
*100 g (3½ oz) black olives, stoned and chopped*
*200 g (7 oz) can tuna in oil*
*100 g (3½ oz) lard, cubed*
*2 egg yolks, beaten*

Put 450 g (1 lb) of the flour on to the table top. Make a hollow in the centre with your fist and put the salt and yeast in the hollow. Mix together and knead with as much water as it takes to make a smooth elastic bread dough, rubbing flour over the table top and your hands. When the dough is smooth and well worked, cover it with a cloth and leave in a warm place to double in size.

Meanwhile, fry the garlic in a little oil, add the tomatoes and a little more oil, cook briefly then remove from the heat. Add the anchovies, capers and olives, then flake in the tuna and mix well.

When the dough has doubled, push it flat on the table and knead in three-quarters of the lard. Set aside a teaspoonful of beaten egg and knead the remainder into the dough. Knead very thoroughly, then tear off one-third of the dough lump, so you have a big and a smaller bit.

Oil a 25 cm (10 inch) cake tin and line it with the bigger piece of dough. Fill it with tomato mixture and cover with the second piece of dough, rolled out thinly. Pinch the

MAKING TOMATO PASTE *This traditional method of drying sieved tomatoes in the sun achieves a dense, 'tomato-ey' concentrate.*

edges together carefully, brush with the reserved beaten egg and the remaining piece of lard, melted, and leave to prove in a warm place for 30 minutes. Bake in a moderate oven (180°C, 350°F, gas mark 4) for 25–30 minutes. Serve the pizza hot, perhaps with green salad.

# RISOTTO RUSTI

## RED WINE AND BORLOTTI RISOTTO

In Lombardy they know just about everything you might need to know about risotto and red wine. This wonderfully rustic risotto is made with lard, beans, onions and dense red wine – some of my personal favourites are Botticino, Buttafuoco or Oltrepò Pavese Barbera.

### SERVES 4

*700 ml (1¼ pints) or more vegetable, chicken*
*or beef broth*
*100 g (3½ oz) lard, butter or ham fat*
*1 large onion, finely chopped*
*300 g (10 oz) risotto rice*
*1 large glass, about 150 ml (5 fl oz), red wine*
*salt and pepper*
*200 g (7 oz) cooked borlotti beans*
*(fresh, dried or canned)*
*50 g (1¾ oz) unsalted butter*
*50 g (1¾ oz) freshly grated Parmesan cheese*

Heat the broth to a slow simmer. In a large pan, heat the lard, butter or ham fat until sizzling softly, then add the onion and cook gently until the onion is a transparent blond colour and soft. Add the rice and fry it carefully, turning it so it is coated in fat.

Pour in the red wine, stir and cook for 5 minutes. Season with salt and pepper. Add the broth and the beans alternately, stirring in a ladleful of broth then a large spoonful of beans. Allow the rice to absorb the broth before adding any more. Continue until the rice has almost cooked, about 25 minutes from the time of adding it to the onion. Take off the heat and stir in the butter and Parmesan cheese. Cover and leave to rest for 2–3 minutes, then turn out on to a serving dish and serve.

# RISO ALLA SICILIANA

## SICILIAN RICE

This delicious rice dish brings together all the most typical flavours of Sicilian cuisine. It should be lukewarm when served but never refrigerated. You can add more tomatoes fried in olive oil and flavoured with marjoram if you like. It's delicious served as part of a summer buffet with other vegetable dishes. As in many Sicilian dishes, it is the layering of the three main parts of the dish which is important, mixing them all up together would completely change the nature of the dish.

### SERVES 4

*1 large salted anchovy or 2 anchovy fillets*
*300 g (10 oz) long-grain rice*
*1 onion, finely chopped*
*about 5 tablespoons olive oil*
*1 tablespoon white wine vinegar*
*1 wine glass, about 150 ml (5 fl oz), white wine*
*juice of 3 lemons*
*½ teaspoon mustard*
*½ teaspoon tomato paste*
*3 firm ripe tomatoes, halved, seeded and cubed*
*50 g (2 oz) black olives, stoned*
*a large pinch of dried marjoram*

Bring a large saucepan of salted water to the boil. Put a plate on top of the pan, covering the water. Lay the anchovy on the plate and mash it with a fork. It will dissolve smoothly with heat. When the anchovy has melted, remove the plate and add the rice to the water and cook until tender.

Meanwhile, in a small saucepan, fry the onion in 2 tablespoons olive oil. When the onion is golden and soft, sprinkle the vinegar over it and allow it to evaporate for 2 minutes. Add the wine, lemon juice, mustard, anchovy and tomato paste. Mix with great care, then sieve once to make a smooth sauce.

Drain the rice and spread it out on a warmed serving platter. Pour the sauce over it and sprinkle with a little salt and pepper. While the rice cools slightly, fry the tomato cubes quickly in about 3 tablespoons olive oil for 1 minute, then mix in the olives and the marjoram. Pour them over the rice and sauce, then serve.

# BRUDERA

## SAUSAGE – MEAT RISOTTO

It is impossible to make any of the many dishes of Italian peasant cuisine that use fresh pig's blood unless you live near a pig farmer or are brave enough to go to the slaughterhouse yourself. I know it sounds primitive, but I promise you the end result is delicious and very nutritious.

### SERVES 4–6

*¼ of a boiling fowl or equivalent chicken trimmings*
*450 g (1 lb) pork ribs (as meaty as possible)*
*salt*
*1 onion, finely sliced*
*100 g (3½ oz) butter*
*75 g (2½ oz) Italian sausage-meat*
*freshly ground black pepper*
*400 g (14 oz) risotto rice*
*1 wine glass, about 125 ml (4 fl oz), fresh pig's blood, still warm (optional)*
*freshly grated Parmesan cheese, to serve*

Put the boiling fowl or trimmings and the ribs in a large saucepan with a little salt and 1.5 litres (2½ pints) water and bring to a slow boil, then simmer for about 2 hours. Remove meat and leave to cool; keep the broth hot.

Fry half the onion and half the butter with the sausage-meat. Scrape the meat off the pork ribs and chicken and mince it once, or chop very finely, then mix with the onion and sausage. Season with black pepper. Cover and simmer for 15 minutes.

Fry the remaining half onion in the remaining butter until the onion is soft. Add the rice and stir well. Fry it lightly, then start adding the hot broth, a ladleful at a time, stirring it into the rice each time. After 15 minutes, stir in the blood, if using, or the cooked meats with the onion. (If you are using the blood do not add the meat at this stage.) Add a little more broth and cook for the final 5 minutes.

Turn out on to a platter, scatter the meat on top if not already added, and serve with plenty of Parmesan cheese. If you do use the blood, you will find the dish turns a lovely brick red colour and changes completely in flavour. Serve with a good bottle of Barolo or Barbaresco.

RISO ALLA SICILIANA

## RISI E BISATO

### RISOTTO WITH EEL

This superb risotto, which is made with eel, comes from the Veneto. Serve it with a Piave Verduzzo.

SERVES 4

*300 g (10 oz) fresh eel (can be a fresh water or sea fish)*
*a handful of fresh parsley*
*2 cloves garlic*
*7 tablespoons olive oil*
*salt*
*1 small bay leaf*
*2 teaspoons or more lemon juice*
*300 g (10 oz) risotto rice*
*750 ml (1¼ pints) vegetable broth*
*freshly ground black pepper*
*8 tablespoons cooked peas (optional)*
*lemon wedges to garnish*

Skin, gut and wash the eel then cut into short chunks. Chop the parsley and garlic together, put into a saucepan with the oil and heat gently. Add the eel to the pan and sprinkle with a little salt. Add the bay leaf and lemon juice, cover and cook for about 10 minutes.

Stir in the rice and half the broth, stir and continue to cook, adding more broth as soon as it is absorbed, until the rice is tender. Remove the pan from the heat, stir in plenty of freshly ground black pepper, and the cooked peas if using. Leave, covered, for 2 minutes.

To serve, tip out on to a serving dish and spoon into a mound or flattish cake shape; garnish with lemon.

## POLENTA SULLA SPIANATORA

### POLENTA ON THE TABLE

The origins of this dish go way back in the dark mists of time, but maybe there is a place for the meaning behind the dish — now more than ever. The ritual arising from eating the food in this way is that gradually trenches and gullies open up in the polenta as everybody picks out the best bits, until at last the culmination of the meal is all the forks touching one another — a symbol of friendship and fraternity. The atmosphere surrounding this meal is very jovial and fun loving — try it for yourself and see. The best kind of table is one that is much battle-scarred and imbued with flavours of a thousand and one meals prepared and eaten on it with love and care.

SERVES 8

*1 large onion, chopped*
*1 large carrot, chopped*
*1 large stick celery, chopped*
*3 cloves garlic, peeled and chopped*
*a handful of fresh parsley and basil, mixed*
*5 tablespoons olive oil*
*1 litre (1¾ pints) passata or sieved tomato*
*16—20 sausages (preferably Italian)*
*salt and pepper*
*450 g (1 lb) polenta (yellow cornmeal)*
*1.75 litres (3 pints) boiling water*

Fry the onion, carrot, celery, garlic, and herbs in the olive oil in a large pan until the onion is transparent. Pour in the passata, add the sausages and season with salt and pepper. Cover and simmer for about 1½ hours.

After the first hour, pour the flour into the boiling water in a large pan in a steady stream. Stir constantly and cook at a slow bubble for about 30 minutes. The polenta is cooked when it comes away from the sides of the pan.

Tip the polenta straight on to the table, right in the centre. Spread it out sideways a little, then tip the sausage mixture on top and spread that around a little. Now hand each person a fork and let them eat what is on the table directly in front of their place.

# POLENTA PASTISSADA

## LASAGNE-STYLE POLENTA

Polenta is a staple in northern Italy, where it is as popular as pasta is in the south. The basic method of cooking it is below. Many households keep cold, cooked polenta ready for frying or turning into other dishes.

This old traditional country dish from the Veneto makes a wonderful golden cake. Polenta is cut into slices, then arranged in layers with a tomato and veal sauce, cheese and butter and baked like lasagne.

### SERVES 8

*340 g (12 oz) polenta (yellow cornmeal)*
*1.2 litres (2 pints) boiling water*

### SAUCE

*20 g (¾ oz) dried porcini (or other dried mushrooms)*
*1 onion, chopped*
*1 carrot, chopped*
*1 stick celery, chopped*
*150 g (5 oz) butter*
*150 g (5 oz) veal steak, trimmed and cubed*
*½ wine glass, about 75 ml (2½ fl oz), dry white wine*
*225 g (8 oz) fresh ripe tomatoes, peeled, seeded and chopped*
*½ teaspoon tomato paste*
*salt and pepper*
*75 g (2½ oz) Parmesan cheese*
*75 g (2½ oz) chicken livers, cleaned and chopped*

KITCHEN UTENSILS *Beautiful and natural materials such as wood, copper and cast-iron are favoured in the kitchen.*

In a large saucepan add the polenta flour to the boiling water and stir quickly to a smooth texture. Cook for 30 minutes, stirring almost constantly until the polenta comes away from the side of the pan. Tip it out on to a board and let it set slightly. When it is cool and solid, slice it into 1 cm (¾ inch) thick strips.

Cover the dried mushrooms with lukewarm water and leave to soak for about 15 minutes.

Meanwhile, put the chopped onion, carrot and celery in a pan with about one-third of the butter and fry until soft. Add the meat and brown all over. Pour in the wine and boil rapidly for about 5 minutes to evaporate the alcohol. Add the tomatoes and tomato paste, and season and stir. Cover and simmer for 30 minutes.

Drain the mushrooms, chop if large and stir into the pan. Cook for a further 30 minutes. Cut the Parmesan cheese into flakes with a cheese slicer. Cook the chicken livers quickly in about 30 g (1 oz) butter.

Butter an ovenproof dish large enough to take the slices of polenta and the meat and tomato sauce. Arrange a layer of polenta slices on the bottom, pour a little sauce over and scatter a few flakes of cheese over it. Cover with another layer of polenta slices, dot with butter and a few chicken livers and more flaked Parmesan. Cover with another layer.

Continue in this way with alternate layers – meat and tomato sauce and Parmesan or chicken livers, butter and Parmesan, ending with Parmesan and butter. Bake in a hot oven (200°C, 400°F, gas mark 6) for 20–25 minutes. Serve at once with a full-bodied red wine.

## POLENTA DI PATATE

### POTATO POLENTA

This is an unusual recipe because the polenta is not cooked, simply combined with cooked, mashed potato. In a peasant community 3 kg (7 lb) of potatoes would probably be needed to serve eight and the sauce would be less generous!

SERVES 5—6

*1.5 kg (3⅓ lb) white floury potatoes*
*salt and pepper*
*4 tablespoons polenta (yellow cornmeal)*
*large onion, finely sliced*
*30 g (1 oz) butter*
*cooking oil*
*300 g (10 oz) thick cut streaky bacon, cut into cubes*
*about 300 g (10 oz) mozzarella, emmenthal or*
*stracchino cheese cut into cubes*

Cook the potatoes in salted boiling water until soft. Mash them with a solid potato masher, preferably in a copper bowl, certainly in a metal one (the perfect tool for this job is an Irish masher – rather like a culinary shelalagh!).

When they are smooth, add the polenta flour a little at a time, and keep mashing until the potato comes away from the sides with no difficulty. This procedure should take about 30 minutes. To keep the potato polenta hot, either hold the metal bowl over a very low heat or mash off the heat and keep returning to the heat every few minutes to re-heat. The first option is better if you can manage it.

In a separate pan, fry the onions with the butter and oil until golden, then add the bacon and fry until crisp. When the polenta is smooth and very hot, tip the cheese cubes and the fried ingredients into the metal bowl and mix thoroughly. Tip the whole thing out on to a big wooden board and smooth over.

To serve, using a long piece of thick, clean white thread cut through the polenta 'cake' like cutting through cheese with a wire. Cut into big chunks, put a chunk on each plate and serve with a bowl of pickles and cooked beans tossed in a sharp oil and vinegar dressing.

## CANEDERLI DI FEGATO

### LIVER DUMPLINGS

Strictly this is not a pasta dish, but any Italian would understand its being included here, for it is cooked and served 'in brodo', like so many stuffed pastas. A rosé wine is the traditional drink to serve with these dumplings. I suggest the delightful Casteller from the vineyards of the Trentino in the north, where this dish is enjoyed.

SERVES 6

*450 g (1 lb) stale white bread, 2 or 3 days old,*
*not sliced*
*400 g (14 oz) calf's liver or chicken livers*
*a handful of fresh parsley, finely chopped*
*1 stick celery, finely chopped*
*1 small onion, finely chopped*
*a sprig of fresh marjoram, finely chopped*
*salt and pepper*
*a pinch of grated nutmeg*
*grated rind of 1 lemon*
*1 tablespoon olive oil*
*2 eggs*
*200 g (7 oz) fine white flour*
*100 ml (3⅓ fl oz) milk*
*1.5 litres (2½ pints) good meat or vegetable broth*

DRYING MAIZE *Dried maize, traditionally part of farmhouse cooking is now mainly used as chickenfeed. Corn-fed chicken tastes especially good!*

Cut the bread into thin slices, then cube it. Mince the liver to a pulp. Mix together the vegetables, herbs, bread and liver. Season with salt, pepper and nutmeg then add the lemon rind, olive oil and eggs and stir thoroughly. Add the flour and the milk and stir vigorously until you have a thick, smooth mass.

Bring a large pan of water to the boil, shape the dough into balls about the size of a baby's fist. Slide them into the water and cook gently for 20 minutes.

Meanwhile, heat the broth. When the dumplings are ready, ladle the broth into 6 bowls. Scoop out the dumplings from the water with a slotted spoon and divide them equally between the 6 bowls. Served at once with a sprinkling of extra parsley and marjoram, and more broth if you like.

# GRANO AL RAGU

## CORN GRAIN WITH MEAT AND TOMATO SAUCE

This was originally a cheap peasant dish, made from dried maize. The maize was soaked for 12 hours then cooked in fresh water for 3–4 more, until soft, then served with sauce. The meat from the sauce can be served separately as a second course with a green vegetable or salad.

### SERVES 6

6–8 corn-on-the-cob or 1.2 kg (2½ lb) frozen or
canned, drained corn kernels
50 g (1¾ oz) fresh parsley
2 cloves garlic
large pinch chilli powder
large pinch grated nutmeg
115 g (4 oz) pecorino or Parmesan cheese
570 g (1¼ lb) pork steak, in one slice
75 g (2½ oz) streaky bacon, rindless
2 tablespoons olive oil
1 tablespoon pork dripping
½ glass, about 75 ml (2½ fl oz), red or white wine
450 g (1 lb) canned tomatoes, seeded
salt and pepper

Chop the parsley and garlic together, then mix in the chilli and nutmeg. Chop 30 g (1 oz) pecorino into tiny cubes and add them too. Beat the pork to flatten as much as possible, then spread the mixture over it. Cover with the bacon, roll it up on itself like a Swiss roll and tie securely with fine string.

Choose a small flameproof casserole or saucepan into which the meat fits neatly. Heat the oil and dripping and brown the meat on all sides, then add the wine. Cook for 5 minutes, then add the tomatoes and season with salt and pepper. Cover and simmer for about 2 hours, stirring the tomato occasionally and adding water if it appears to be drying out.

Cook the corn kernels — for about 10–12 minutes if fresh. When tender, drain and dress the corn with the sauce from the casserole. Serve with a small slice of meat — though originally this would have been part of another course. Scatter with plenty of grated pecorino.

# MEAT, POULTRY, GAME, SALUMI

*Meat, always a delicacy in the farmhouse kitchen, is made the most of in special festive dishes, and is the base for some delicious everyday casseroles and hotpots.*

STUFATO DI MANZO CON PATATE *(p 61)*

I HAVE TRIED TO CREATE a balance between those recipes that use animal offal and those which use the more familiar cuts of meat. The Easter lamb dish is a typical example of the use of special meat to make a special dish. In complete contrast is the dish of stewed pig's trotters, which might, for example, be served with polenta as a complete meal. Offal is very much a part of any peasant cuisine, and I hope that the more adventurous cooks will be tempted by the rich Italian tradition, which my selection of recipes can only hint at.

In the south there is a tradition of one-pot cooking – all the stews and soups and broths are prepared in one blackened pot which hangs over the fire. Here, the pot would also be used to prepare a meaty concoction with plenty of sauce. The sauce would be used to dress a dish of pasta as a first course, and the meat would be saved to eat as a second course with vegetables.

The flavour of a free-range chicken that has scratched around and decided on its own lunch is completely different from a factory farm hen – the colour and texture are worlds apart. I still feel happier eating wild meat (game) than meat which comes from an animal that has been fed all kinds of things it probably would not have chosen to eat had anybody asked it.

Rabbit is a very emotive subject when you translate it into food, more so than the less attractive creatures. But overcome your feelings and you will discover a delicious and tasty meat that is extraordinarily versatile. It is especially good in a tomato-rich casserole with plenty of black olives, or in the Sardinian recipe on page 77.

You will notice that pork crops up quite frequently in this section. This is because pigs are popular to keep as a family animal on a small farm. All year long the beast can be happily tended, allowed to roam freely and eat more or less what it likes. In the autumn it is slaughtered ceremoniously and most is cured to last through the winter, in the form of prosciutto, salami, mortadella, sausages such as Zampone and Cotechino for the New Year's Eve celebrations and so on. Although this is changing, most housewives in Italy tend not to be happy about eating or cooking pork during the summer months for fear of illness, for refrigeration is a relative newcomer to their lives.

# STUFATO DI MANZO CON PATATE

## BEEF STEW WITH POTATOES

This is actually made like a pot roast except that the beef is rolled up around a filling of pork belly flavoured with red wine and fresh parsley. It's a delicious, heart-warming dish, perfect for suppers, on cold winter evenings.

### SERVES 6

*85 g (3 oz) pork belly strips, cut into small cubes*
*salt and pepper*
*500 ml (18 fl oz) red wine*
*2 tablespoons chopped, fresh parsley*
*900 g (2 lb) rump steak in one piece, flattened out and trimmed*
*6 tablespoons olive oil*
*2 tablespoons plain flour*
*8 tablespoons passata or sieved tomato*
*about 300 ml (½ pint) good meat stock*
*900 g (2 lb) potatoes, peeled and cubed*

Put the pork belly into a bowl and season very thoroughly, then cover with the red wine. Leave to marinate for 1 hour. Remove the pork belly with a slotted spoon, reserving the marinade, and roll each piece in parsley. Arrange the pieces over the steak and roll up the meat, securing it with the 4 wooden cocktail sticks.

Heat the oil in a flameproof casserole and brown the rolled up meat all over, then remove the meat and set aside. Sprinkle the flour into the hot oil and mix it in to make a roux, then pour in the marinade and mix together. Cook for about 4 minutes or until you can no longer smell the wine evaporating.

Return the meat to the casserole with the tomato passata and 300 ml (½ pint) stock. Season and cover with a sheet of greaseproof paper, then place the lid on top. Simmer for 3 hours, preferably in a warm oven (160°C, 325°F, gas mark 3). Add the potatoes with a little more stock — just enough to cover the contents completely including the potatoes. Return to the oven and cook for a further 25 minutes, or until the potatoes are soft. Serve piping hot with plenty of bread and robust red wine.

# MANZO AL GRAS DE ROST

## BEEF STEWED WITH DRIPPING

This is a delicious way of stewing cheaper cuts of beef which may be tough yet full of flavour. From the foggy plains of Lombardy, where they know all about the rigours of a cold winter, comes the recommendation that you should accompany the stew with plenty of robust, heart-warming red wine and boiled potatoes to mop up the rich meat juices.

### SERVES 4

*800 g (1 lb 10 oz) stewing beef (in one piece)*
*75 g (2½ oz) unsalted butter*
*1 tablespoon plain flour*
*salt and pepper*
*2 tablespoons pork or beef jellied juices, from beneath a joint (not the fat)*
*300 ml (½ pint) good beef stock*

Trim the meat and tie if necessary. Mash the butter with the flour and put it in a heavy flameproof casserole into which the meat fits snugly. Melt the fat until sizzling. Lay the meat in the fat, turning it to brown all over, then season well with salt and pepper.

Add the stock and jellied meat juices, stirring them into the butter until heated through. Cover and cook over a low heat for about 4 hours. Baste the top of the meat with the stock from time to time. Cut the meat into thick chunks and pour the juices from the pot over the meat before serving with boiled potatoes.

61

# TORTINO
# DI PATATE E CARNE

## MEAT AND POTATO CAKE

Originally from Austria, where it is called G'rostl, this dish is a very simple and economical way of using up leftover boiled beef to make a delicious fried 'cake' of meat and potatoes flavoured with chives.

### SERVES 4

*50 g (1¾ oz) butter*
*2 tablespoons chopped fresh chives*
*400 g (14 oz) cold boiled beef, cut into small chunks*
*4 cold boiled potatoes, cut into small chunks*
*salt and pepper*

Heat the butter in a 17.5 cm (7 inch) pan and snip the chives into the butter. Add the meat, potatoes and salt and pepper. Mix together very thoroughly, then cook for 10 minutes, pressing down with a palette knife to create a crisp crust underneath.

Turn the potato cake over by sliding it on to a plate and then tipping it back into the hot pan. Cook until the other side is also just crisp, then serve at once. It is also very good cold and makes an excellent item for a picnic.

# STRACOTTO

## POT-ROASTED BEEF

This delicious, juicy and soft pot-roasted beef is an ancient dish which goes back several centuries in Italian peasant cookery. Originally the pot used to make it in would have been made of glazed terracotta with a tight-fitting lid. In those days no other flavouring ingredients were added; the dish was simply the best quality stewing beef cooked in plenty of robust red wine.

### SERVES 6

*1.5 kg (3 lb) stewing beef in one piece, rolled*
*and tied into shape*
*4 cloves garlic, cut lengthways into strips*
*50 g (1¾ oz) pork dripping*
*1 onion, chopped*
*1 carrot, chopped*
*1 stick celery, chopped*
*85 g (3 oz) butter*
*1 tablespoon tomato purée diluted in about*
*300 ml (11 fl oz) stock, plus extra stock if required*
*salt and pepper*

Pierce the meat with a skewer and insert slivers of garlic into the holes. Mix the dripping with the chopped vegetables, then put this mixture into a deep, heavy pan into which the meat fits. Add the butter and fry the vegetables for 5 minutes. Then add the meat and seal it all over.

Pour in the stock mixture and season with salt and pepper. Cover with a tight lid and cook very slowly for 5 or 6 hours, basting the meat every now and again with more stock and turning it over.

At the end of the cooking time, remove the meat from the sauce. Slice it thickly and arrange on a serving dish, pour over the sauce from the pot and serve at once.

COWS DRINKING AT MARKET-PLACE *A martyred St Sebastian presides over this peaceful scene in the village of Glorenza near the Austrian Border.*

# LESSO RIFATTO
# ALLA SENESE

## BOILED BEEF
## IN THE SIENNA STYLE

This excellent and typically frugal dish, uses up all the odd bits of meat, leftover from making the ever-present meat broths, which are normally rather boring and unimaginative when eaten on their own. It also works very well with the leftovers of a roasted joint, provided that it is fairly plain and unflavoured. In itself it is not very substantial, but it is one of those Tuscan dishes that marries perfectly with the local bean dishes such as Fagioli Stufati (see page 101).

SERVES 4

*450 g (1 lb) leftover boiled beef*
*60 ml (2 fl oz) olive oil*
*300 g (10 oz) onions, finely sliced*
*300 g (10 oz) fresh ripe tomatoes, seeded and coarsely chopped*
*salt and pepper*
*chopped fresh basil or dried basil, to taste*

Slice the meat into thick rounds. Heat the oil in a saucepan, add the onions and fry until golden but soft. Add the meat and the tomatoes and season with salt and pepper.

Sprinkle the basil over the top and cook through until hot and bubbling. Arrange the meat on a serving platter, pour the sauce over it and serve at once.

# SPEZZATINO CON ZUCCHINE E PATATE

## COURGETTES, POTATO AND VEAL STEW

This delicious summer stew from Liguria makes the best use of the fresh, light tasting courgettes and tiny potatoes available in that area. In Italy, where the calves are milk-fed and are killed very young, this would be a quick dish – probably only 30 minutes' simmering with tender meat. But for Northern Europe, where the calves are older, I have allowed extra simmering time.

### SERVES 6

150 ml ($\frac{1}{4}$ pint) olive oil
4 or 5 cloves garlic, sliced
2 sticks celery, chopped
1 large carrot, sliced
1 large onion, sliced
750 g (1$\frac{1}{2}$ lb) stewing veal, cut into cubes
1 large glass, about 150 ml (5 fl oz), dry white wine
450 g (1 lb) new potatoes, scrubbed and washed
about 5 tablespoons chicken, meat or vegetable stock
400 g (14 oz) ripe tomatoes, peeled, seeded and chopped
$\frac{1}{2}$ teaspoon tomato paste
300 g (10 oz) fresh young courgettes, sliced
pinch of dried oregano
salt and pepper

Heat the oil in a heavy-bottomed pan, add the garlic and fry until soft. Add the celery, carrot, onion and veal and brown the meat on all sides.

Pour in the wine and cook for 5 minutes to let the alcohol evaporate, then add the potatoes and the stock. Simmer gently for about 1$\frac{1}{2}$ hours, until the meat is approaching tenderness. Then add the tomatoes, tomato paste, courgettes and oregano. Season and cook gently for a further 20 minutes, adding a little more stock if required. Serve hot with salad and dry white wine.

STRAW WAGON IN TUSCANY *Oxen pull a wagon across a field of stubble in the rolling green hills of Tuscany.*

# TESTINA DI VITELLO AL SUGO

## STEWED HEAD OF VEAL

Sicilians prepare this dish from the boned and rolled calf's head, which is available already prepared in all good butchers' shops. This is then singed over an open flame at home and scraped to remove bristles. It then needs washing and blanching. If you manage to buy a head, ask your butcher to bone and roll it. However, the sauce is so good, and the garnish attractive, that the recipe translates well to the expensive cuts of veal, like shoulder or leg.

### SERVES 4

450 g (1 lb) veal, boned and rolled
salt
1 carrot, cut into 4 pieces
1 stick celery, cut into 4 pieces
1 onion, cut into 4 pieces
2 cloves
1 onion, finely sliced
60 g (2 oz) butter
60 ml (2 fl oz) olive oil
300 g (10 oz) passata or sieved tomato
6 tablespoons milk
4 tablespoons chopped, fresh parsley
rind of $\frac{1}{2}$ a lemon, finely sliced
2 fresh sage leaves, finely chopped

Put the meat in a pan, add a little salt and the carrot, celery, and the onion pieces with the cloves stuck into one of the pieces, and cover with cold water. Bring to the boil, then simmer for 1 hour.

Meanwhile, fry the onion in the oil and butter in a separate pan for about 10 minutes over a low heat, then add the passata. Stir and season, then simmer for about 1 hour, adding the milk halfway through.

Drain the veal and cut it into neat slices, then slide them back into the sauce. Make sure the meat is completely covered in sauce and simmer gently for no more than 10 minutes.

Arrange the meat on a warm serving dish with the sauce poured over it. Scatter the parsley, lemon rind and sage over the top and serve at once with potatoes and a simple vegetable dish.

COUNTRYSIDE NEAR BARRAFRANCA *in the Enna region. The gentle hills, speckled with olive trees and patch-worked with arable land, roll into the distance.*

# AGNELLO ALLA SICILIANA

## SICILIAN LAMB

Like all Sicilian dishes, this one has a good strong flavour. Make sure that the ingredients are evenly distributed in the casserole. The potatoes should soak up all the flavour and grease from the meat. If a lower fat version is preferred, reduce the quantity of lard by half. The ground pepper is a very important ingredient and ideally should be crushed with a pestle in a mortar.

### SERVES 4

*900 kg (2 lb) stewing lamb, cut into chunks*
*4 potatoes, peeled and quartered*
*60 g (2 oz) pork fat or lard*
*1 large onion, cut into 4 pieces*
*4 cloves garlic, chopped*
*1 sprig fresh rosemary*
*salt and plenty of freshly ground black pepper*
*200 g (7 oz) canned tomatoes, chopped and seeded*

Wash and trim all fat from the meat. Arrange it in a casserole with the potatoes, lard, onion, garlic and rosemary. Season with salt and plenty of freshly ground black pepper, then spoon the tomatoes on top. Cover and cook in hot oven (180°C, 350°F, gas mark 4) for 2 hours. Serve very hot with vegetables and bread.

# U'VERDETTE

## EASTER LAMB FROM APULIA

In traditional shepherds' regions it is only natural that dishes made with lamb in all its forms should be the most popular. This dish comes from Apulia – the heel in the Italian boot – but lamb is eaten all over Italy at Easter. The reasons are practical as well as symbolic. The size of the herd must be reduced as summer starts because the heat reduces the grazing available. This delicious Easter lamb dish is very unusual as the cooked meat is finished off with a dressing of eggs and cheese.

### SERVES 4

*800 g (1 lb 10 oz) boned leg of lamb*
*6 tablespoons olive oil*
*1 large onion, sliced*
*1 glass, about 150 ml (5 fl oz), dry white wine*
*450 g (1 lb) peas*
*salt and pepper*
*2 large eggs*
*a handful of grated pecorino cheese*
*a handful of fresh parsley, grated*

Cut the meat into chunks and wash and dry. Heat the oil in a heavy-bottomed saucepan, add the onion and fry until it is softened.

Add the meat and brown all over. Stir in the wine and cook until the alcohol has evaporated. Cover with a tight-fitting lid and cook in a moderate oven (170°C, 350°F, gas mark 4) for about 20 minutes. Add the peas and season with salt and pepper. Cook for a further 25 minutes.

Break the eggs into a bowl and whisk in the cheese and parsley. Remove the lamb from the oven and take off the lid. Pour the egg mixture over the meat, let it stand until the eggs have scrambled, then serve at once.

# AGNELLO ALLA PECORARA

## LAMB SHEPHERD'S-STYLE

From the mountains of the Abruzzi and the timeless villages of the Molise comes this very simple dish of pot-roasted lamb which is allowed to cook in its own fat. Traditionally, a copper pot with two handles is used to cook the meat, but any heavy-bottomed pot that is flameproof will work equally well, provided it has a tight-fitting lid.

### SERVES 4–6

*1 large onion, peeled and left whole*
*20 g (¾ oz) unsalted butter*
*900 g (2 lb) leg or shoulder of lamb, cut into*
*6 pieces*
*salt*
*8 slices coarse bread*

Put the onion and the butter in a heavy-bottomed flameproof casserole. Salt the lamb and arrange the meat in the casserole so that the pieces lie flat on the bottom. Cover and cook over a medium heat for 1 hour. Do not remove the lid while the meat cooks.

To turn the lamb, take the 2 handles firmly in your hands and toss the casserole to turn the pieces over without removing the lid. Turn them about 5 times during the cooking time. Toast the bread in the oven, arrange the meat over the bread and serve at once.

# SALSICCIA ALL'UVA

## SAUSAGES WITH GRAPES

From the region of Umbria, famous for its pork and sausage products, comes this dish of fresh sausages cooked with firm ripe white grapes. It's a lovely combination and the slightly sour quality of the grapes reduces the fattiness of the sausages. Buy the largest grapes possible. Good quality fresh Italian sausages are available from all good Italian delicatessens. Other coarse sausages can be used provided they are made almost wholly of pork.

### SERVES 4

*8 plump fresh coarse pork sausages*
*2 tablespoons olive oil*
*750 g (1½ lb) firm white grapes removed from the stalk*
*and washed*

Wipe the sausages with a clean damp cloth. Prick them all over. Heat the oil in a wide, deep pan and place the sausages in the hot oil. Brown them all over and let the fat run out. Cook for about 6 minutes more, then remove from the pan. Tip out almost all the fat, then return the sausages to the pan and add the grapes.

Cook over a high heat for 5 minutes, turning the grapes over with a wooden spoon being very careful not to break or split the skins. Serve with the grapes.

# PUCCIA

## CABBAGE AND PORK SAUSAGE POLENTA

It is hard to describe this delightful winter warmer from Piedmont. It's a cross between a meat pudding and a stew – although neither of those words make it sound particularly appetizing! It is really delicious, a comforting and tasty combination of pork sausages, green cabbage and polenta, dressed with butter and cheese.

### SERVES 4—8

*450 g (1 lb) green savoy cabbage, washed and cut into*
*thin strips*
*450 g (1 lb) coarse pork sausages*
*salt*
*200 g (7 oz) polenta (yellow cornmeal)*
*50 g (1¾ oz) plain white flour*
*50 g (1¾ oz) unsalted butter*
*freshly ground black pepper*
*freshly grated Parmesan cheese, to taste*

Put the cabbage in a wide heavy-bottomed pan with the sausages, pricking the sausages to make the juices run. Add a little salt, cover, and cook over a very low heat for about 20 minutes.

Meanwhile, mix the polenta and flour together in a pan big enough to hold everything in the recipe. Add enough water to make a thick paste about the same consistency as porridge, stirring constantly so that the polenta won't be lumpy. It should be a runny consistency rather than stiff. Cook the polenta for 20 minutes, stirring all the time.

Add the cabbage and sausages and cook together for 5 minutes, then season with pepper. Ladle into soup plates to serve, putting the sausages on top if you can, and scattering dabs of butter over the polenta and cabbage mix. Sprinkle with plenty of grated Parmesan cheese and eat at once.

SALSICCIA ALL·UVA

# CECI CON LA ZAMPINA DI MAIALE

## CHICK PEAS WITH PIG'S TROTTERS

The original version of the dish called for tempia di maiale (above the eyes) which is the fattiest part of the pig, and the result is an extremely heavy, greasy dish. The idea behind dishes like this was to provide internal central heating for peasants living in icy-cold conditions. In this updated version the trotters are used instead, making a more tasty and nourishing dish. The timing is for modern chick peas too.

### SERVES 6–8

*150 g (5 oz) dried chick peas*
*1 teaspoon bicarbonate of soda*
*2 pig's trotters, split and washed*
*900 g (2 lb) pork loin, cubed in big chunks*
*1 large carrot, cut into cubes*
*2 large sticks celery, cut into sections*
*3 small onions, peeled and quartered*
*a sprig of fresh rosemary*
*a sprig of fresh sage*
*salt and pepper*
*pickled peppers*
*pickled gherkins*
*pickled onions*
*freshly grated Parmesan cheese, to serve*

Cover the chick peas with cold water, add the bicarbonate of soda and soak for 24 hours. Drain and wash in cold water.

Put the trotters, meat, vegetables and herbs in a large casserole, cover with water. Add salt and pepper and simmer slowly for 4 hours until the meat is falling off the trotters and the fat has almost turned to jelly.

About 1½ hours before the trotters will be ready, cover the chick peas with plenty of fresh water and boil slowly, without salt, over a low heat without removing the lid.

Add the chick peas to the meat and vegetables and cook for a further 30 minutes, then serve. The meat is usually taken out and served with pickles, while the remaining mixture is served as a very thick soup, sprinkled with grated Parmesan cheese.

# FASUI CUL MUSET

## BEANS WITH COTECHINO SAUSAGE

Cotechino, called Muset in Friuli dialect, is a deliciously spicy, rich and soft sausage, traditionally served on New Year's Eve with lentils. In the Friuli, it is eaten throughout the winter months and often cooked with beans, onion and butter in this delectable, simple recipe. Cotechino sausage is available at good Italian delicatessens; the cooking instructions vary according to the brand.

### SERVES 4

*200 g (7 oz) dried beans (any variety you prefer)*
*1 large red onion or 2 smaller ones, finely sliced*
*50 g (1¾ oz) butter*
*3 tablespoons light olive oil*
*6 fresh sage leaves, chopped*
*salt and pepper*
*1 cotechino sausage*

Soak the beans overnight in cold water, drain and wash them. Cover in clean cold water and boil very fast for 10 minutes, drain and return to pan. Cover with fresh water and simmer slowly without a lid.

Fry the onion in the butter and oil until the onion is crisp and golden. Pour the onion and the fat into the bean pot and stir, sprinkle in the sage and season to taste. Continue to cook for 1½–2 hours, depending on the size of the beans.

Cook the cotechino separately according to the instructions on the packet, then slice it into thick rounds. Add the sliced sausage to the beans and heat through for 5 minutes. Serve on warm plates with plenty of red wine, such as a Merlot or Cabernet.

## COPPA SENESE

### FRESH SIENNESE SALUME

This is a preserved meat — a salume — for immediate consumption; it isn't one you can hang up and use over several months. Ideally it should be eaten within 3 days of preparation. It is not cooked a second time before it is eaten. You will need to make yourself a sausage bag about 20–25 cm (8–10 inches) long and 7–10 cm (3–4 inches) wide out of doubled muslin or cotton sheeting to hold the sausage ingredients in shape.

#### SERVES ABOUT 10

*the ears, head, trotters, tail and trimming of skin*
*from a freshly butchered pig*
*30 g (1 oz) salt per 900 g (2 lb) raw pig*
*4 g (⅛ oz) ground black pepper per 900 g (2 lb) raw pig*
*4 cloves garlic, finely chopped*
*grated rind of 1 orange*
*grated rind of 1 lemon*
*½ teaspoon mixed spices*
*½ teaspoon ground cinnamon*
*1 teaspoon fennel or caraway seeds*

Trim and clean all the parts of the pig. Scald the hairy bits over an open flame and scrape off the hairs and hard skin with a sharp knife. Wash it very carefully, then weigh it all together and make a note of the weight.

Bring a large pan of water to the boil, then immerse all the pieces of pig in the water. Bring back to the boil, then turn off the heat. Leave the pan undisturbed until the following day.

The next day, pour off the water and replace with fresh water, bring back to the boil and simmer for about 3 hours. Remove from the heat and pick off all the meat and fat, discarding all the bones.

Chop all the meat coarsely, then put it all into a bowl and add the salt and pepper according to the weight you recorded when it was raw. Mix in the garlic, grated orange and lemon rind, the spices and the seeds. Stir together very thoroughly, then spoon it all into a cloth bag. Tie it up firmly with clean string and hang it up to dry in an airy place for 24–48 hours.

When it's firm and dry, remove the bag and slice the meat into rounds. Serve with plenty of bread and wine as a snack or antipasto.

## ANIMELLE AL PROSCIUTTO

### SWEETBREADS WITH HAM

This robust offal dish is typical of the provincial areas around Rome. It is traditionally served with fresh peas or artichokes with melted butter and plenty of parsley, which adds a welcome touch of colour.

#### SERVES 4

*570 g (1¼ lb) lambs' sweetbreads*
*salt*
*75 g (2½ oz) prosciutto crudo, coarsely chopped*
*1 onion, finely sliced*
*1 tablespoon olive oil or 15 g (¼ oz) butter*
*5 tablespoons good broth*
*30 g (1 oz) butter*
*½ tablespoon plain flour*
*freshly ground black pepper*

Carefully peel the membrane from the sweetbreads, cover with cold water and leave to soak for 3 hours. This will ensure they remain perfectly white. Drain and toss into boiling water for 3 minutes. Drain again and rinse under cold water, then pat dry and slice into neat rounds.

Fry the prosciutto and onion in the olive oil or butter in a saucepan for 5 or 6 minutes. Add the sweetbreads and reduce the heat to as low as possible. Fry them very carefully, turning them once, for a total of 10–12 minutes. Add about three-quarters of the broth as they cook.

Remove the sweetbreads and arrange them on a warm dish. Mash the 30 g (1 oz) butter and the flour together and stir into the pan juices, with the remaining stock. Season with pepper. Stir together and cook to a smooth sauce. Pour the sauce over the sweetbreads and serve at once, with a green vegetable to garnish.

VINEYARDS IN AUTUMN *(p 72) Italian vines grow vertically up poles not horizontally as in France. In the autumn, the vine leaves turn a spectacular red-gold.*

# TRIPPA DI
# MONGANA ALLA CANEPINA

## VEAL TRIPE
## COOKED IN THE CANEPINA STYLE

The most important ingredient of this traditional winter dish from the Marche is the ham bone, which imparts a delicious flavour. It is a dish from the province of Ancona and varies slightly from one village to another. The final result is a rich, rib-sticking concoction which is served with big slabs of coarse country-style bread, lightly toasted, then sprinkled with olive oil. The best kind of tripe is calf's, although lamb's tripe can be used.

*SERVES 4—6*

*900 g (2 lb) calf's honeycomb tripe (or lamb's tripe)*
*1 onion, finely chopped*
*2 cloves garlic, finely chopped*
*1 large carrot, finely chopped*
*1 stick celery, finely chopped*
*a large pinch of dried marjoram*
*peel of 1 lemon, finely chopped*
*3 strips pork belly, cubed*
*1 ham bone*
*1 tablespoon tomato paste*
*salt*
*country-style bread*
*freshly grated Parmesan cheese, to serve*

74

Wash the tripe in several waters, trimming off loose pieces. Scald it by pouring boiling water over it. Put it in a saucepan, cover with cold water, bring to the boil and cook for about 20 minutes. Drain, wash again, then cut into cubes.

In a deep, heavy-bottomed pan, put the chopped onion, garlic, carrot, celery, dried marjoram, lemon peel and pork belly and fry together slowly until the vegetables are soft. Add the tripe and the ham bone and cover with water. Stir in the tomato paste and salt to taste and simmer for 2 hours, adding more water as required. Serve with plenty of bread and grated Parmesan cheese.

FARMHOUSE *Utility is the farmer's watchword — he won't be too bothered by his flaking stucco walls.*

# POLLO ALLA TOSCANA

## TUSCAN-STYLE COUNTRY CHICKEN

A deliciously simple and very typically Tuscan chicken casserole. Serve with mashed potatoes and a green vegetable and more white wine.

SERVES 4

*30 g (1 oz) dried porcini*
*about 300 ml (10 fl oz), warm chicken stock*
*1.5 kg (3 lb) chicken, preferably maize fed,*
*jointed into 8 pieces*
*85 g (3 oz) unsalted butter*
*about 50 ml (1¾ fl oz), olive oil*
*1 glass, about 150 ml (5 fl oz), dry white wine*
*salt and pepper*
*225 g (8 oz) canned tomatoes, sieved*
*1 tablespoon plain flour*

Wash and pick over the mushrooms carefully. Cover with half the stock and leave to soak for about 15 minutes.

Heat one-third of the butter with the oil in a flameproof casserole. Add the chicken pieces and brown them all over. Add the wine and season with salt and pepper. Cook for 5 minutes to evaporate the alcohol, then add the tomatoes. Stir in the rest of the stock and the mushrooms. Cover and cook over a low heat for 40 minutes.

Remove the chicken from the pot and keep warm. Mash the remaining butter with the flour and mix it into the liquid in the casserole. Cook until the sauce is thick and smooth, then pour it over the chicken and serve at once.

# POLLO RIPIENO ALLE NOCI

## STUFFED CHICKEN WITH WALNUTS

From the mountains of Trentino comes this delicate boiled boned chicken with its delicious stuffing of walnuts, nutmeg and pine nuts.

### SERVES 6

*1.5 kg (3 lb) chicken, boned*
*2 stale white bread rolls, all crust removed*
*milk*
*60 g (2 oz) shelled walnuts*
*60 g (2 oz) pine nuts*
*150 g (5 oz) marrow from beef shin bones*
*the giblets from the chicken*
*salt and pepper*
*1 heaped tablespoon Parmesan cheese*
*¼ teaspoon grated nutmeg*
*1 or 2 eggs, beaten*

Bone the chicken by slitting the skin along the backbone and then working a sharp knife between the flesh and the carcass. Remove all the bones you can see, scraping the flesh off them and always working from the inside. Your butcher can do this for you.

Cover the bread with milk and leave to soak for about 15 minutes. Meanwhile, blanch the walnuts in boiling water and remove the skins. Put them in a blender or food processor and grind them; a food processor makes a coarser mix. Cook the giblets in boiling water for 5–6 minutes then remove the neck bone and process the flesh to a fine pulp with the beef marrow. Remove the bread from the milk and squeeze it dry in your hand. Process the bread with the giblets. Mix in the ground nuts, pine nuts and nutmeg, seasoning to taste with salt and pepper. Stir in a little egg spoonful by spoonful, adding more if the mixture feels at all dry.

Put this filling inside the boned chicken and sew it up along the back with fine string or thread. Put the chicken in a large saucepan, cover with water, cover and simmer over a medium heat for about 1 hour. Serve hot or cold, carved across in slices.

**UNSHACKLED CART BY AN OLD STONE WALL** *The chicken pecking around this old wooden cart looks ready to stand in for the usual team of oxen.*

# CONIGLIO A SUCCITTU

## STEWED SARDINIAN RABBIT

This deliciously vinegary rabbit stew is often served cold – in fact many Sardinians claim it is much better cooked and left to cool, then eaten the following day. This is also an excellent way to cook hare or venison.

### SERVES 6

*1.5 kg (3 lb) rabbit, jointed*
*1 rabbit's liver*
*50 ml (1¾ fl oz) olive oil*
*1 large onion, finely chopped*
*4 cloves garlic, chopped*
*50 g (1¾ oz) capers, washed and dried and*
*finely chopped*
*salt*
*½ glass, 60 ml (2 fl oz) red or white wine*
*4 tablespoons wine vinegar*

Wash and dry the rabbit. Finely chop the trimmed liver. Heat the oil in a heavy-bottomed pan, add the rabbit joints and cook until browned all over.

Mix the chopped liver, onion, and garlic together with half the capers and stir into the pan. Cook over a medium heat for 20 minutes, then season with salt. Add the vinegar to the wine with about 60 ml (2 fl oz) water and pour over the meat. Add the remaining capers, cover and cook gently until tender, up to 45 minutes, checking that it is not burning. Serve hot or cold.

# TORESANI ALLO SPIEDO

## PIGEONS WITH JUNIPER BERRIES

Toresani is the Venetian word used to describe a particular variety of pigeon, also called Torraioli. I have found this dish works with any type of pigeon and that the essential part of the dish is that you must cook on a spit, either in the oven or outside over an open fire or barbecue.

SERVES 4

*10 juniper berries*
*2 dried bay leaves*
*salt and pepper*
*4 tablespoons olive oil*
*1 rosemary branch, about 15 cm (6 inches) long*
*4 small, plump, gutted and cleaned pigeons*
*130 g (4¼ oz) pork fat (fresh fat, skinned and removed from the back in a sheet)*

Crush the juniper berries in a mortar along with the bay leaves and some salt and pepper. Add the olive oil and mix together.

Dip the rosemary branch in the flavoured oil and paint the inside of each bird with the oil. Cut the fat into 4 strips and wrap a strip around each bird with the oil. Secure it in place with string, then thread each bird on to the spit and cook over a medium heat for 30 minutes, basting with the remaining oil.

Just before serving remove the string around the fat. Traditionally, this is a dish served with polenta (page 55) that has been sliced and fried quickly in a pan with a little oil until brown on both sides.

TORESANI ALLO SPIEDO

# FISH
# AND SEAFOOD

*Italy is proud of her fish cookery. Her
peninsular coastline and well-stocked rivers
and lakes yield a bounty of choices for rich,
savoury stews and bakes, or simple grills
and frys.*

BURIDDA DI PESCE FRESCO *left (p 90)* FRITTELLE
DI BACCALA *right (p 86)*

I CAN REMEMBER FISHING TRIPS as a child. We would go out at sunset from the beach — in those days the water was clear and green as glass — and as the sun slipped lazily down into the sea, the mountains behind the house would turn glowing garnet red and magenta and violet, the last rays of the sun just catching the furthest snowy peaks before it disappeared. We would set off through the tiny waves on a pattino, which for anybody who doesn't know is a pedalo with very long and narrow oars. Rowing one is an art form in itself — once learnt, never forgotten. — and the control you have over it is vital to a fishing expedition. One person would row (or two children) and two people would let the nets go slowly into the water from the bow. The nets would be coiled neatly in buckets on the two sharp tips of the bow and you would have to straddle the wood and use two hands to empty the nets into the waters. All around us fish would jump and splash and on a good night we would see dolphins in the far distance, or a shoal of really huge fish leaping away to safer waters.

When the last centimetre of net had gone into the sea, all that you could see were the black-flagged buoys marking the places where the nets began and ended. We would row back to shore, light a fire and grill sausages over the red hot embers. When the deckchairs and sand were soaked with dew we would wend our way home, pattino secure on its rollers and nets hopefully already filling up. And there was never the sound of a discotheque to disturb our sleep! Dawn came too soon, the mountains this time a brilliant yellow and red, the sea deep purple and warm and clearer than ever. Nobody was on the beach so early, except other fishermen, mothers with very young babies taking the sea air before the heat, old people paddling in the peace before the arrival of the crowds, and the odd rider galloping along the shingle.

Once the nets had been drawn in on board the pattino, it was always the children's job to keep the nets and the fish in the buckets rather than back in the water where they very much wanted to be. And then we would crouch on the shore line, threading the net through from left hand to right hand, removing anything edible on the way and tossing it into another bucket. Squid would peck and pinch, sting rays would send us yelling into the sea if we touched their blue spots and got an electric shock, crabs would hang on to thumbs for dear life — but exhausted and fishy we would return home by 7.30 a.m., bringing lunch for everybody (there never seemed to be less than 20 people there for any meal!), a collection of baby soles, red mullet, sometimes bass and silver mullet, lots of squid and 'cicale di mare' (sea crickets) and a whole variety of wonderful fresh fish.

In any case, the recipes in this section are all family favourites, and none of them should give you any trouble, except perhaps the stockfish/salt cod which can be off-putting to buy — it looks exactly like a very old and dried up floor cloth of a disreputable household! I promise you that once reconstituted and cooked it will taste delicious. If you simply cannot face it, chunks of monkfish or very thick cod will work just as well in all the stockfish recipes.

The couscous recipe may also require a certain amount of devotion — I have shown you the laborious method for making authentic couscous from semolina, and it is certainly not one for the faint-hearted. Even original Moroccan couscous will take you an hour to cook in a special couscousière, but don't despair, there is a widely available instant version which you can cook in the pan in ten minutes (see glossary).

# VONGOLE IN PORCHETTA

## CLAMS WITH HERBS AND WINE

For this quintessential Ligurian starter, you can use any small molluscs — even cockles and winkles — or small mussels. The most important thing is that they should be absolutely fresh.

SERVES 4

*1.8 kg (4 lb) small clams or other small molluscs*
*a handful of fresh fennel or dill*
*a large sprig of fresh rosemary*
*50 ml (1¾ fl oz) olive oil*
*3 cloves garlic, peeled*
*salt and pepper*
*½ glass, about 60 ml (2 fl oz), dry white wine*
*1 heaped tablespoon tomato paste, diluted in 60 ml*
*(2 fl oz), warm water*

Clean and wash all the molluscs very carefully. Chop the fennel or dill. Remove all the leaves from the rosemary and chop them.

Heat the oil in a large saucepan, add the garlic and herbs and fry for 2 minutes, then add the clams and season very generously. Pour over the wine and cook with the lid on for 5 minutes to evaporate all the alcohol.

Add the diluted tomato purée, stir and cook for as long as it takes to cook the seafood through — certainly no more than 5 minutes. Serve with plenty of crusty bread.

# POLPI IN GALERA

## IMPRISONED OCTOPUS

Small octopus or squid are needed for this Tuscan antipasto — small enough to gut without cutting off the head.

SERVES 4

*800 g (1 lb 10 oz) smallish octopus or squid*
*100 ml (3½ fl oz) olive oil*
*2 cloves garlic, chopped*
*a handful of fresh parsley, chopped*
*salt and pepper*

Clean and gut the seafood, removing eyes and beaks and inner sacs. Heat the oil in a flameproof casserole that will just hold them all. Add the garlic and parsley and fry for about 6 minutes, then add the seafood and season. Cover and cook for no more than 30 minutes, shaking the casserole every now and again to prevent sticking.

# PURPETTI DI NUNNATA

## WHITEBAIT FRITTERS

This is a delightful way of cooking whitebait, in the Sicilian tradition, using the freshest of ingredients.

SERVES 4

*570 g (1¼ lb) very fresh whitebait or similar tiny fish*
*a small fistful of fresh parsley, chopped*
*2 cloves garlic, finely chopped*
*1–2 eggs*
*salt and very little pepper*
*oil for deep frying*

Wash the fish and dry it carefully. Mix the fish, parsley and garlic together in a bowl. Beat the eggs with a minimum amount of salt and pepper, then mix this into the fish. Stir together very carefully to make a thick mass.

Heat the oil in a large pan and fry the mixture in spoonfuls, making little piles. Scoop them out 3 or 4 at a time and serve at once without waiting for them all to be ready. Do not add lemon juice as is often done.

# SEPPIE COI PISELLI

## SQUID WITH PEAS

Peas are a very popular vegetable in the whole of the Lazio, turning up in various combinations of fish and meat as a kind of stew. Traditionally cuttlefish are used, but tender young squid, cut into neat white strips, are ideal and easier to buy.

SERVES 4

*900 g (2 lb) squid (450 g (1 lb) if bought ready trimmed and sliced)*
*salt*
*3 cloves garlic, chopped*
*5 tablespoons olive oil*
*a handful of fresh parsley, chopped*
*750 g (1½ lb) unshelled or 175 g (6 oz) frozen peas*
*150 ml (¼ pint) passata or sieved tomato*
*pepper*

Clean the squid unless you have bought them ready cleaned. Use the head to pull out the sac inside the body. Cut off the head and tentacles (the tentacles can be used for soup) just behind the eyes and discard all this with the body contents. Flex the body slightly to pop the transparent internal stiffener out (this is a white cuttle bone, if you buy cuttlefish). Peel off the dark skin outside as much as possible, using salted hands.

With a pair of scissors, split the squid open completely and open out flat. Remove any odd bits of sac and wash thoroughly under running water. Cut into long neat strips with a very sharp knife. Wash again and dry in a clean cloth.

Fry the garlic in the olive oil until golden, then add the parsley and the peas. Stir together carefully, then add the squid and passata. Season with salt and pepper and cook for about 15 minutes, taking care not to overcook it as the fish can become very rubbery. Stir often and add a little water if necessary.

Serve very hot with thick slices of coarse Italian bread.

FISHING ON LAGO LARIO, *in the province of Como. Italians are especially fond of their lake fish which are the basis of many local specialities.*

# BACCALA CON I PEPERONI

## SALT COD WITH PEPPERS

From joyous Naples comes this lovely bright dish of dried cod stew with green and yellow peppers, finished off with tomato and chilli for extra impact. Salt cod is often paired with peppers, which are strong enough to stand up to its own positive flavour.

SERVES 4

800 g (1 lb 10 oz) dried salt cod
flour
oil for deep frying
5 yellow and green peppers
100 ml (3½ fl oz) sunflower oil for shallow frying
2 large onions, finely sliced
450 g (1 lb) fresh ripe tomatoes, peeled,
seeded and chopped
½ teaspoon tomato paste
a handful of fresh parsley, chopped
½ dried red chilli
salt

Soak the fish overnight in cold water, changing this several times – a bowl standing in a sink under a running tap is ideal. This reconstitutes the fish and removes salt, and the soaking time depends on how long the fish is to be cooked later. At least 24 hours are needed if the subsequent cooking is brief.

Wash and skin the fish and remove any bones. Cut it into even chunks discarding thin edges, and toss them in flour. Heat the oil for deep frying in a pan and fry the fish until crisp and golden. Drain on kitchen paper.

Hold the peppers one at a time, over a flame turning them around so the skin blisters and blackens, then peel off the transparent skin with a sharp knife. Cut the peppers in half, remove the seeds and slice them into strips.

Heat the oil for shallow frying in a separate pan, add the onions and fry gently until soft and mushy. Stir in the tomatoes, paste, parsley and chilli and season with salt. Add the fried fish and peppers, cover and cook for 10 minutes. Serve hot or cold.

FISHERMEN LANDING THEIR CATCH *Red mullet can be seen in the box in the foreground and one large grey mullet in the batch of smaller silver fish.*

# FRITTELLE DI BACCALA

## SALT COD FRITTERS

In regions that are a long way from the coast, like lovely Umbria, stockfish often crops up on the menu as a tasty and cheap standby. True stoccafissa is a whole dried cod, in its natural shape. It's very leathery and needs beating to break down the fibres, then soaking for 36–48 hours in several changes of water. It's a medieval way of preserving that was safe in summer heat. Baccalá, which is cod opened flat, salted and dried, is easier to buy and slightly quicker to prepare. In Perugia they cook it like this, simply dipped in batter and deep fried in olive oil, then serve it with lemon segments for squeezing over.

SERVES 4

*800 g (1 lb 10 oz) dried salt cod, soaked for
at least 24 hours*
*1 large egg, beaten*
*6 tablespoons plain flour*
*150 ml (¼ pint) milk (more or less may be necessary)*
*575 ml (1 pint) olive oil*
*2 lemons, cut into 8 segments*

Wash and skin the fish and remove any bones. Cut the fish into neat chunks.

Mix the egg with the flour and enough milk to make a thickish batter. Heat the olive oil in a deep pan. Dip the fish in the batter and then fry until crisp and golden. Drain carefully on kitchen paper, then serve piping hot with the lemon segments.

# BACCALA ALLA POTENTINA

## SALT COD STEWED WITH SULTANAS AND OLIVES

Dried salt cod is transformed into a delicious meal by combining it with olives, sultanas, onions and tomatoes. This recipe comes from the desperately poor region of Basilicata in the arch between the heel and toe of the Italian peninsula. There is a similar recipe in Naples using squid, if these are any easier to get than baccalá. Cook them for 15 minutes only.

SERVES 4

*800 g (1 lb 10 oz) dried salt cod, soaked overnight*
*75 g (3 oz) sultanas*
*115 g (4 oz) black olives*
*60 ml (2 fl oz) olive oil*
*1 large onion, sliced thinly*
*2 tablespoons tomato paste, diluted in 150 ml (5 fl oz)
warm water*

Wash and skin the fish and remove any bones. Cut the fish into neat chunks. Cover the sultanas in warm water and soak them for no more than 10 minutes. Stone the olives and cut them in half.

Heat the oil in a heavy bottomed pan, fry the onion until soft. Then add the pieces of fish and turn them carefully to brown them on all sides.

Stir in the sultanas, olives and tomato liquid, taking care not to break up the fish, then cook over a very low heat for 1 hour, stirring occasionally. Serve hot, with fried peppers.

# SARDELE RIPIENE

## STUFFED SARDINES

Although originally from the Veneto, this recipe for cooking fresh sardines is in use all around the Mediterranean with slight variations on the basic theme. It makes a substantial antipasto or first course dish.

SERVES 4

*8 large fresh sardines*
*3 tablespoons fresh breadcrumbs*
*3 tablespoons freshly grated Parmesan cheese*
*1 tablespoon chopped fresh rosemary or*
*1 teaspoon dried rosemary*
*2 tablespoons chopped fresh parsley*
*2 cloves garlic, very finely chopped*
*salt and pepper*
*olive oil*

Remove the heads and guts, then slit the fish open lengthways. Wash and leave to drain very thoroughly. Pat dry with a cloth or kitchen paper.

Mix together the breadcrumbs, Parmesan cheese, herbs and garlic. Add a little seasoning and enough oil to make a smooth paste. Fill each fish with some of this paste and push them back into shape.

Oil an ovenproof dish and arrange the fish in a single layer in the dish. Sprinkle with a little salt and pepper, dribble a little oil on top and bake in a moderate oven (180°C, 350°F, gas mark 4) for about 15–20 minutes. Serve very hot.

# BURIDDA DI PESCE FRESCO

## LIGURIAN FRESH FISH STEW

In this tasty fish stew from the seaside region of Liguria, all the flavours of the sea are blended together with fresh tomatoes, herbs and wine to make a truly memorable dish.

SERVES 6

*1.2 kg (2 lb 7 oz) mixed fresh fish, including plaice fillets, turbot, red mullet, scorpion (rascasse), monkfish and rockfish*
*450 g (1 lb) mixed shellfish, such as prawns, shrimps and scampi, shelled*
*900 g (2 lb) onions, sliced*
*450 g (1 lb) fresh tomatoes, peeled, seeded and chopped*
*¼ teaspoon tomato paste*

*1 large glass, 150 ml (5 fl oz), dry white wine*
*salt and pepper*
*a handful of fresh parsley, chopped*
*2 tablespoons dried oregano*
*olive oil*

Wash and trim all the fish and shellfish. Grease a flameproof casserole large enough to take all the ingredients. Scatter a layer of sliced onions on the bottom. Cover with a layer of fish and shellfish. Season with salt and pepper then cover with some of the chopped tomato.

Repeat the layering with onions, a little oil, then fish and shellfish and finally tomato and the paste. Sprinkle the herbs over the top. Pour in the wine very carefully, then dribble olive oil over the top. Cook, uncovered, over a very low heat for about 35 minutes or until the liquid in the casserole has thickened to a soupy consistency. Serve hot or just tepid with plenty of bread.

## LUCCIO IN STUFATO

### STEWED PIKE

Pike is one of those awkward fish that are difficult to cook as their flavour and texture are somewhat limiting. In the lakes of Lombardy they are plentiful and are cooked in this flavourful stew with red wine and vegetables. The recipe works with any rich, meaty fish – tuna is ideal, and does not have the awkward little bones of a pike.

SERVES 4

*1 pike, gutted, about 570 g (1¼ lb)*
*50 g (1¾ oz) butter*
*3 tablespoons olive oil*
*225 g (8 oz) small onions, chopped*
*225 g (8 oz) young tender carrots*
*2 large sticks celery, finely chopped*
*plain flour*
*1 large glass, about 150 ml (5 fl oz), robust red wine*
*salt and pepper*
*250 ml (8 fl oz) cold water*

Wash the pike and remove as many scales as possible drawing a knife down it. Leave to drain.

Heat the butter and oil in a flameproof casserole, add the vegetables and fry until soft. Coat the fish with flour, add to the vegetables and cook until brown all over. Pour over the wine and season thoroughly. Cook over a high heat for 5 minutes to evaporate the alcohol, then add the water. Cover and cook over a gentle heat for 1 hour. Carefully remove the fish and lay it on a warm platter. Sieve the vegetables in the casserole and pour the resulting smooth sauce over the fish. Serve at once.

## ANGUILLA ALLA NUORESE

### NUORO-STYLE EEL

Eel is an acquired taste for many people, but cooked properly it can be really delicious and loses much of its muddy aftertaste. This recipe comes from Nuoro in Sardinia. The fish can be skinned before use or not, but the fins must all be removed.

SERVES 4

*2 tablespoons olive oil*
*900 g (2 lb) eel, cut into chunks*
*3 cloves garlic, peeled and chopped*
*900 g (2 lb) ripe fresh tomatoes, peeled,*
*seeded and chopped*
*¼ teaspoon tomato paste*
*salt and pepper*
*a handful of fresh parsley, chopped*
*a handful of fresh basil, chopped*

Skin the eel if there is a fat layer beneath the skin, and cut it into chunks. Heat the oil in a heavy-bottomed pan, add the eel chunks and brown them on all sides, then remove from the oil and set aside.

Put the garlic into the oil and fry for 2 minutes, then add the tomatoes and paste, stir together and season. Cook for about 10 minutes, then return the eel to the pan. Cover and cook for 5 – 8 minutes, depending on the thickness of the fish. Uncover, scatter the herbs over the fish and serve straight from the pan.

SARDINIAN BOATMAN *(p 90) A Sardinian peasant punts a boat laden with reeds across the tranquil waters.*

RIFUGI AND ALLOTMENT *(p 92) These whitewash cabins are shelter for the days when farming is not close to home. They are set in an allotment with vegetables and fruit trees.*

## TROTELLE AL POMODORO

### TROUT IN TOMATO SAUCE

Wonderfully fresh and tender young trout, simmered in a fresh tomato sauce laced with olive oil, parsley and garlic make up this fine dish from the mountains of the Abruzzi and the Molise. Do not use a large trout with a thick skin.

SERVES 4

*30 g (1 oz) chopped fresh parsley*
*1 clove garlic, chopped*
*50 ml (1¾ fl oz) olive oil*
*450 g (1 lb) ripe fresh tomatoes, peeled, seeded*
*and chopped*
*½ teaspoon tomato paste*
*salt and pepper*
*4 small trout, total weight about 800 g (1 lb 10 oz),*
*gutted and cleaned*

Put the parsley, garlic and olive oil in a pan large enough to take all the fish, then fry for 1–2 minutes. Add the tomatoes and paste and mix together. Season with salt and pepper, then simmer for about 5 minutes.

Place the trout in the tomato mixture and spoon the tomato over them so they are semi-covered. Cover and cook for about 20 minutes, then serve with a dry fresh white wine like Frascati.

## BORETO ALLA GRAISANA

### GRADO-STYLE TURBOT

Always accompanied by the soft and creamy white polenta which is eaten locally, this superbly simple dish allows the fine flavour of the fish to shine through.

SERVES 3–4

*about 50 ml (1¾ fl oz) olive oil*
*3 whole cloves garlic*
*450 g (1 lb) turbot, cleaned, in one piece*
*salt and pepper*
*good quality wine vinegar*

Heat the oil in a saucepan large enough to take the fish. Add the garlic and fry until dark brown. Remove the garlic and lay the fish in the hot oil. Sprinkle with salt and pepper and a little vinegar. Cook for 5 minutes, spooning the hot oil over the fish.

Pour in enough water to come halfway up the fish. Continue cooking for 10–12 minutes or until the fish is cooked through. Serve hot with polenta.

## MUGGINE AL SALE

### MULLET BAKED IN SALT

Any large fish with a thick scaly skin will work perfectly in this recipe, but it must be freshly caught and fairly big – over 1 kg (2¼ lb) at least. It can serve up to ten people depending on the size of the fish. Don't be put off by the distinct lack of other ingredients: fish cooked like this will taste of the sea and of the fish – nothing else will come between it and you!

SERVES 4

*1 kg (2¼ lb) ungutted, unscaled mullet, dorade or other*
*large scaly fish*
*rock salt*

Wash the fish but do not cut it or touch it in any other way. Cover the bottom of an ovenproof dish large enough to take the fish comfortably with a 7.5 cm (3 inch) layer of rock salt.

Place the ungutted fish on the top and cover it completely with more salt to a depth of 7.5 cm (3 inches). Press down hard on the salt with the heel of your hands so as to create a compact cover.

Cook in a moderately hot oven (190°C, 375°F, gas mark 5) for 1 hour, then crack the salt crust and remove salt and skin in one go so as to reveal a fragrant fish. Serve at once. You can remove the salt at the table as an added attraction, if wished.

MUGGINE AL SALE

# CUSCUSU

## SICILIAN COUSCOUS

The Arab dish of couscous is very popular in eastern Sicily where housewives prepare it regularly and therefore have all the correct equipment. They start by making the couscous itself, which is then steamed and served with a delicious fish stew, which is also called couscous. You can buy dried North African couscous ready-made and this will need the same long cooking time. If you use 1 kg (2¼ lb) instant couscous, soak it for 10 minutes in boiling fish broth, then fork it, to separate the grains. Or serve the fish couscous with rice. In all these cases I would compensate by adding the saffron to the fish stew.

### SERVES 6

#### HOME-MADE COUSCOUS
*200 g (7 oz) fine grain semolina*
*200 g (7 oz) thick grain semolina*
*½ teaspoon powdered saffron*
*100 ml (3½ fl oz) hot water*
*60 ml (2 fl oz) olive oil*
*1 tablespoon ground black pepper*
*a large pinch of ground cinnamon*
*a large pinch of grated nutmeg*
*fish stock or water, to steam*

#### FISH STEW
*2 cloves garlic, chopped*
*50 ml (1¾ pt) olive oil*
*a handful of fresh parsley, chopped*
*1 large onion, sliced*
*1 bay leaf*
*3 canned tomatoes, seeded and chopped*
*1.2 kg (2½ lb) assorted fish such as mackerel, cod, eel, cleaned and gutted*
*salt and pepper*

Mix the semolinas together very carefully. Dissolve the saffron in hot water, then put 1 tablespoonful of the diluted saffron into a large wide bowl with a handful of semolina. Rub the semolinas up the sides and across the bottom of the bowl, making it granular (pieces no bigger than a peppercorn), then scoop out the couscous and spread on a clean tablecloth.

Go through all the semolina this way, a small amount at a time with a little bright yellow saffron water. Leave it spread out like this to dry out.

Pour the stock or water into a pan and put a large metal colander on top. Wrap a cloth around the colander where it meets the top of the pot so as not to lose any of the steam in the next stage of cooking.

Tip the granular couscous into the colander and pour the olive oil over it. Mix together with your hands and then lay a heavy clean cloth on top of the grains and a lid on top of that. Bring the liquid to the boil and let it boil very slowly, for 1½ hours so the couscous cooks in the steam coming through the holes of the colander.

After about 1 hour, start the fish stew. Fry the garlic and the oil in a large pan or flameproof casserole with the parsley and onion for about 3 minutes, then add the bay leaf and tomatoes. Cook for about 5–6 minutes, then add all the fish and season with salt and pepper. Add about 600 ml (1 pint) water, enough to cover the fish, then cover with a lid and simmer for about 25 minutes.

When the couscous is ready, tip it into a bowl, sprinkle about 5 tablespoons of the liquid used for steaming over the grains and stir them well to separate them. Cover with a lid, wrap the bowl up in a woollen cloth or towel and put it in a warm place to swell. Overall, it will need about 1 hour to swell.

When the fish is ready, scoop out the pieces with a slotted spoon and keep in a warm place. Pour the fish broth through a strainer – there should be about 500 ml (18 fl oz). Pour half of this into another jug and let it cool a little, so that it thickens to make the final sauce. Meanwhile, the couscous needs sprinkling with as much fish broth as it will absorb every 15 minutes, and stirring each time to make sure the grains are not sticking together. Keep it warm all the time.

After an hour, dress the couscous with the pepper, cinnamon and nutmeg and a little of the reserved fish broth. Arrange the hot fish on top and serve at once.

OLD HOUSE AT A QUAYSIDE *This old house with its Arab-style windows could easily date back to medieval times.*

# VEGETABLES AND SALADS

*Vegetables are treated with imagination and respect in Italy, with the staples — aubergines, tomatoes and peppers — given as much attention as the more unusual swiss chard, scorzonera, and turnip tops.*

VRUOCCOLI AFFUCATI *(p 102)*

Anybody who has ever visited an Italian market, even in the tiniest little village, or the smallest green grocer's shop, will have been amazed at the extraordinary variety of vegetables and types of salad available. The most basic Trattoria will serve you an 'insalata mista' with at least 4 kinds of lettuce or vegetables. Plain boiled vegetables are usually considered something to be eaten only when one is under the weather.

As you can tell by a glance at these recipes, vegetables are treated with imagination and respect in Italy. Raw cabbage sautéed in a pan with olive oil, chillis and garlic is really delicious, and there are countless recipes for aubergines, peppers and courgettes. Even the humble cauliflower, in our opening picture, is turned into a dish of true excellence. The Italians have a rich array of choice – both in recipes and ingredients. The cook will prefer to shop on a daily basis, so that the produce used is very fresh and at market she will keep her eyes peeled for the stall selling the best-looking artichokes, then shop around for good-looking spinach and choose her tomatoes from yet another stall.

Vegetables have always marked the passage of the seasons, and although hot-house production is now changing that to some extent, for me, tomatoes, peppers, courgettes and lettuce still represent the summer, tender young spinach and peas tell me spring is finally here, celery and artichokes and mushrooms are part of the autumn, just as leeks and cabbage and potatoes are part of the winter.

At home in Tuscany we would grow almost all the produce required for the summer and it was sheer delight to pick the sun-warmed tomatoes, tiny green beans and brilliant emerald courgettes with their bright orange flowers. Everything was fertilized with chicken and rabbit manure, or manure begged off a local farm. Even if we bought vegetables, they would be from a local small-holding. We would no more dream of eating tomato salad in winter time, than eating polenta with pork sausages in August. Winter was the time for pumpkin and cabbage, beans and chick peas. We knew that you cannot grow proper tomatoes, which really taste like tomatoes, without the sun.

In southern Italy the tomato is called Red Gold, because it is one of the main local industries. There are endless fields of plum tomatoes, just ready to be picked and canned, and exported all over the world. They have had real sun and may well exceed your local fresh ones in flavour.

In the north they are very fond of potatoes, cabbage and beetroot – all three prosper both in the fields and the kitchen. In the areas close to the Austrian border, sauerkraut is very common and popular. In central Italy, they favour vegetables like spinach, chard, cardoons, peas and artichokes. Regions like Lazio and Umbria cook quantities of these in lots of deliciously imaginative ways. Asparagus are popular everywhere, but the best are said to be those grown in Lombardy – short, fat and purple.

To my surprise I find that many people are unaware of Italy's tradition of vegetable cookery – personally I feel that vegetables are as representative of Italian cooking as pasta. I have tried to give an even balance of recipes from all round the country in this section. The recipes are very much personal favourites and most of the vegetables should prove easy to find even if you are not in Italy. I do hope you enjoy them.

# FAGIOLI STUFATI

## STEWED BEANS

If you are lucky enough to find fresh cannellini beans then you will get the full benefit of this recipe and will realise why Tuscans are affectionately known as bean eaters. If fresh beans are unavailable, use dried ones if possible, or canned ones only as a last resort and after rinsing them carefully under running water. In some parts of the region, chunks of tuna or strips of pickled herring are added.

SERVES 4

*900 g (2 lb) fresh cannellini beans or 450 g (1 lb)*
*dried, soaked overnight, or 3 × 430 g (15 oz) cans*
*4 sage leaves*
*salt and pepper*
*virgin olive oil*
*juice of 1 lemon*

Shell the fresh beans and place them in a flameproof terracotta pot. If using soaked, dried beans, bring them up to the boil in fresh water, then drain and rinse carefully. If using canned beans, rinse and drain. Cover fresh or soaked, dried beans with 3 times their volume of fresh water. Add the sage leaves and plenty of salt and pepper. Stir and cover.

Simmer the beans on a very low heat, well below boiling point, for up to 4 hours. Keep an eye on them after the first hour. If the temperature is too high, they could easily cook through too soon and go on to be horribly mushy. Strictly canned beans are already cooked, but at a low temperature they can be stewed gently in a little covering water for 30 minutes to impregnate them with the flavour of the sage. The ideal is that the beans should exactly absorb their water and then be dressed in the cooking pot. If they cook for a full 4 hours, they could absorb 4 times their own volume of water. But if this doesn't go quite as planned, and they are cooked before the water has gone, drain them and return to the pot.

Dress with plenty of olive oil, the lemon juice and adjust the seasoning if necessary. Serve hot.

# SCORZONERA IN UMIDO

## STEWED SCORZONERA

This unusual-looking vegetable, with its dark-brown, long, tapering root is a crisp white inside. It is actually very healthy and sweet tasting. In Liguria they cook it with egg yolks and onion to make a substantial vegetable dish. If you can't get scorzonera, salsify, which is a very similar — though unrelated — vegetable, could be used.

SERVES 4

*800 g (1 lb 10 oz) scorzonera or salsify*
*juice of ½ lemon*
*1 onion, finely chopped*
*a handful of fresh parsley, finely chopped*
*3 tablespoons olive oil*
*salt*
*1 tablespoon plain flour*
*about 650 ml (1 pint 3 fl oz) vegetable stock*
*3 egg yolks, beaten with juice of another lemon*

Scrape the scorzonera and drop it into a basin of cold water mixed with the lemon juice. It otherwise discolours in an unpleasant way.

Put the onion and the parsley in the olive oil in a medium-sized saucepan and fry over low heat until the onion is transparent. Drain and dry the scorzonera and cut into pieces the size of a small finger. Add to the pan, stir and fry gently for 5 minutes.

Sprinkle in the flour and stir again, adding the stock. Cover and simmer for 20 minutes, checking occasionally that it is not catching. When the scorzonera is cooked, check the amount of liquid — you need about 400–425 ml (14–15 fl oz). Pour the egg and lemon mixture all over the top and allow the sauce to thicken for 2–3 minutes before serving hot as a light second course. It also makes an excellent accompaniment to sliced, boiled meat.

## PISELLI IN BARDINO

### STEWED PEAS WITH GARLIC

In the generous-hearted Marche, not even the simple pea escapes being flavoured with lots of rich ingredients and textures. Fresh peas taste much better than canned or frozen peas whatever you do to them but this recipe will enliven frozen or canned peas. Buy about 1.4 kg (3 lb) peas in the pod to get 450 g (1 lb) after shelling.

These peas make a popular 'contorno' for many easy Italian sautéed dishes, for example veal escalopes, or fried chicken. More often, though, contorno means a side dish that is so associated with a main dish that it invariably appears with it – in the way that roast potatoes are part and parcel of a British roast.

SERVES 4

*450 g (1 lb) shelled peas, or canned or frozen peas*
*1 large onion, chopped*
*2 cloves garlic, chopped*
*75 g (2½ oz) butter*
*salt*
*a large pinch of dried oregano*
*150 ml (¼ pint) beef, chicken or vegetable stock*

If using fresh peas, shell them and put them in a bowl of cold water to soak. Fry the onion and the garlic slowly in butter until the onion is transparent, then add the drained peas and sprinkle with salt and oregano. Add a little bit of stock. Cover tightly and simmer very slowly for 30 minutes, stirring occasionally. Frozen peas will take 15 minutes. Serve very hot.

## VRUOCCOLI AFFUCATI

### STEWED CAULIFLOWER

Cauliflower is very popular in Sicily and crops up in all sorts of recipes. The local vegetable has a brilliant emerald green colouring and a much stronger flavour than your average cauliflower, but even the whitest and most bland vegetable will be revived after being stewed in red wine with olives, anchovies, onions and cheese!

SERVES 4–6

*800 g (1 lb 10 oz) cauliflower, divided into florets*
*1 large onion, finely sliced*
*3 tablespoons olive oil*
*3 salted anchovies, filleted and washed*
*55 g (2 oz) pecorino or Parmesan cheese,*
*chopped coarsely*
*12 black olives, stoned*
*salt*
*1 glass, about 115 ml (4 fl oz) red wine*

Blanch the cauliflower in boiling water for 60 seconds. Drain and set aside. Fry the onion in the olive oil. In Italy a flameproof terracotta pot is used, which can then go straight to the table. Chop the anchovies and add half to the onion, then add 1 tablespoon of the cheese and 4 chopped olives.

Cover this mixture with cauliflower florets. Chop the remaining olives and scatter a few over the cauliflower, add a little anchovy and dust with cheese. Sprinkle with salt, cover with more cauliflower, then more olives, anchovies, cheese and a little olive oil. Continue layering until you have used up all the ingredients. Cover with the red wine, sprinkle with a last dribble of olive oil and cover with a close-fitting lid. Place on the stove to simmer very slowly for about 45 minutes. This is an ideal dish for the slowest corner of a solid-fuel cooker. Or if you have a heat diffuser plate, use it – the temperature should be well below boiling. Do not stir or disturb the layers.

Serve hot or cold with plenty of coarse country-style bread or garlic bread made with olive oil.

FRESH VEGETABLE MARKET *Peaches, melons, red peppers, courgettes and beautiful plum tomatoes – these freshly-grown crops are as flavoursome as they are colourful.*

# CIME DI RAPE STUFATE

## STEWED TURNIP TOPS

SERVES 4

*1.8 kg (4 lb) turnip tops or spinach*
*salt and pepper*
*2 cloves garlic*
*3 bay leaves*
*75 ml (2½ fl oz) olive oil*
*1 large glass 150 ml (5 fl oz) rosé wine*

Nothing is ever wasted in a peasant household, whatever is not eaten by the family will be used up by the animals. But this is not the case with the humble turnip top, which is so delicious it is considered too good for the animals. In Apulia they are especially fond of this vegetable and it turns up in all sorts of recipes, often accompanying pasta. This recipe uses garlic, rosé wine and bay leaves to make a very tasty dish. If you haven't got turnip tops, try using sliced turnips or another similar green vegetable such as spinach or beetroot leaves.

Wash and trim the turnip tops or spinach and then cook them in a covered pan with just the water that adheres to the leaves. As they cook, push the leaves aside and remove all the water that forms as they cook, as this is bitter and would spoil the flavour. When there is no more water, add the salt and pepper, garlic cloves, bay leaves, oil and wine. Stir and cook for a further 15 minutes.

# CARCIOFI CON PATATE IN UMIDO

## STEWED ARTICHOKES WITH POTATOES

This lovely Sardinian dish is one of my all time great favourites. It makes a vegetarian main course.

### SERVES 4

*6 globe artichokes or 12 Jerusalem artichokes*
*juice of 1 lemon*
*olive oil*
*2 cloves garlic, chopped*
*a handful of fresh parsley, finely chopped*
*6 potatoes, peeled and cut into the same size chunks*
*salt and pepper*

Peel off the outer leaves if using globe artichokes and trim round the base with a knife. Remove all spines that cover the base beneath the soft inner leaves and cut into 4. Drop into a basin of cold water mixed with the lemon juice. Alternatively, peel Jerusalem artichokes, cutting them into chunks of roughly the same size, and drop them into water with lemon juice.

Heat the oil in a large pan, add the garlic and the parsley and cook for a minute. Add the artichokes and brown them all over. Add a little water, season and cover. Cook very gently for about 30 minutes for globe artichokes, if they are large, 20 minutes for Jerusalem artichokes, adding the potatoes 20 minutes before the end. Add a little water if necessary while cooking, but the finished dish should not be watery.

# LA PEPERONATA

## STEWED PEPPERS

This is the quintessential Sicilian dish, although I have heard people say it comes from bizarre places like Piedmont. The erotic, pulpy, fleshy and juicy pepper, be it red, green or yellow, comes first and foremost from this part of Italy where it was introduced from Latin America along with chocolate and coffee. Real peperoni experts claim that the very best ones are from Calabria, where indeed their texture and size verge on the obscene. But the glorious island of Sicily is rich with bright vegetable dishes like this one, many of which have the flavoursome green Sicilian olives added to make the dish inimitably Sicilian. If peperoni dishes exist in Northern Italy, then it is because they have been introduced by southern immigrants going north in search of well-paid factory work — but here under the southern sun is where the peperoni bring colour and glitter to the poorest kitchens.

### SERVES 4

*4 juicy fat peppers*
*3 large onions, sliced*
*5 tablespoons olive oil*
*300 g (10 oz) fresh ripe tomatoes, seeded and quartered*
*½ teaspoon tomato paste*
*salt*
*3 tablespoons wine vinegar*
*75 g (2½ oz) green olives, stoned and chopped*

Wash the peppers, cut them in half and remove all the seeds and the inner membranes. Cut them in half again — or in strips, if they seem very large — and set aside. Fry the onions in the oil until just soft, then add the tomatoes and tomato paste, and the peppers. Stir and season with salt.

When the peppers are sealed all over, sprinkle in the vinegar and add the olives. Stir well, then cook until the peppers are just cooked, not mushy. Serve hot or cold, with a main course dish or on their own.

PRIEST AND PARISHIONER *(p 104) Seeking out the best fresh vegetables is as much a part of the daily round for the priest as it is for most of his congregation.*

SUNFLOWER FIELD *(p 106) Sunflower oil is a great Italian export, and the fields of flowers make a splash of colour.*

# MELANZANE AL FORNO

## BAKED AUBERGINES

From Apulia comes this deliciously summery aubergine dish. It's got all the flavours of the south – capers, olives, pecorino cheese and of course the velvety rich, Eastern texture and taste of the wonderful aubergine.

SERVES 4

*4 smallish aubergines*
*4 tablespoons fresh breadcrumbs*
*4 tablespoons grated pecorino or Parmesan cheese*
*55 g (2 oz) black olives, stoned and chopped*
*5 tablespoons olive oil*
*salt and pepper*
*a handful of fresh parsley, finely chopped*
*a handful of capers, washed and chopped*
*a handful of dried breadcrumbs*

Cut the aubergines in half lengthways. Very carefully scoop out the pulp with a small spoon. Chop the pulp and prepare as in vegetable section of glossary. Mix it up with the fresh breadcrumbs and the cheese. Mix in the olives and fry this mixture in half the oil for 5 minutes.

Meanwhile, drop the 8 half aubergines into a pan of boiling salted water and cook for 5 minutes. Stir the parsley, capers and remaining oil into the fried mixture. Taste and season generously.

Drain and dry the halved aubergines very carefully, then spoon in the filling mixture. Arrange the filled aubergines in an oiled ovenproof dish and scatter the dried breadcrumbs on the top. Bake in a hot oven (200°C, 400°F, gas mark 6) for 20 minutes. Serve hot or cold as an excellent antipasto or as part of an all-vegetable meal.

# SPINACI ALLA ROMANA

## ROMAN-STYLE SPINACH

In the Lazio, they grow the widest variety of vegetables anywhere in the country. La Campagna Romana has been Rome's market garden for many centuries. Their spinach is especially sweet in this delectable and original recipe.

SERVES 4

*55 g (2 oz) sultanas*
*900 g (2 lb) fresh spinach*
*55 g (2 oz) unsalted butter*
*2 tablespoons olive oil*
*1 clove garlic, crushed*
*55 g (2 oz) pine nuts*
*salt*

Soak the sultanas in warm water for 15 minutes, then drain. Meanwhile, wash the spinach very carefully, trim it and cook it without liquid in a covered pan until soft. Leave it to cool, then squeeze it dry with your hands.

ITALIAN STREET MARKET *Concentration can be read on the faces of the shoppers as they pursue the best and freshest buy.*

Melt the butter in a pan with the oil, add the garlic and fry it until crisp, then discard the garlic. Add the pine nuts and toss until brown then remove. Add the dry spinach and the sultanas to the pan, tossing the spinach with 2 forks to cover it with the butter and oil. Stir in the pine nuts and salt to taste. Heat through, tossing with the forks, for 5–10 minutes, then serve at once.

# COSTE AL POMODORO

## SWISS CHARD WITH TOMATO

Swiss chard is a very popular vegetable throughout Italy but particularly in the provinces around Rome. Swiss chard has an unmistakable flavour and texture and is very easy to grow. It also is one of those vegetables which is attractive enough to grow as an ornamental edible in a border. If you really cannot get hold of chard, large cos lettuce leaves are the closest possible alternative.

SERVES 4

*800 g (1 lb 10 oz) Swiss chard or large dark green*
*cos lettuce leaves*
*60 ml (2 fl oz) olive oil*
*2 cloves garlic, slightly crushed*
*3 salted anchovies, or 6 anchovy fillets canned in oil*
*6 canned tomatoes, seeded*
*salt and pepper*

Pull the dark green chard leaves off their heavy white stalks and put the leaves in a pan with plenty of boiling water. Cook for about 8 minutes. Alternatively, blanch the cos leaves. Drain and dry, then chop very coarsely into wide strips.

Heat the oil in a large pan, add the garlic and fry until the garlic is brown, then discard it. Add the anchovies and the tomatoes. Mix and mash these ingredients into the oil, stirring it all together, then add the chard or lettuce. Turn it over in the sauce and season with salt and pepper. Heat through for 5–10 minutes, then serve hot.

MOTORBIKE WITH VEGETABLES *This useful little machine is the more industrious version of the Vespa and is known as an Ape (bee). It is ideally suited to transporting the produce from the smaller farms.*

# VERZOLINI DELLA VIGILIA

## CHRISTMAS EVE CABBAGE

A very different Christmas speciality for the night before Christmas when it's traditional not to eat meat in Italy. It is a rustic, simple and tasty dish, consisting of stuffed cabbage leaves stewed in tomato sauce, from the province of Parma. Serve 4–5 each as a starter, or as a vegetarian main course with salad.

### MAKES 2 DOZEN STUFFED CABBAGE LEAVES

*570 g (1 lb 4 oz) tender small leaves from a*
*large cabbage*
*75 g (2½ oz) stale white bread*
*6 tablespoons milk*
*225 g (8 oz) freshly grated Parmesan cheese*
*3 eggs, beaten*
*115 g (4 oz) dried breadcrumbs*
*salt and pepper*
*3 tablespoons olive oil*
*30 g (1 oz) butter*
*1 onion, finely chopped*
*8 canned tomatoes, sieved*
*1 tablespoon tomato paste*
*stock*

Soak the stale bread in the milk for about 10 minutes. Wash the cabbage leaves. Bring a pan of water to the boil and cook the cabbage leaves for about 8 minutes, then drain them and lay them out flat on a worktop. Choose the 2 dozen best leaves and chop the rest finely.

Squeeze the bread dry, mix with the Parmesan cheese, eggs, dried breadcrumbs and season generously. Stir in the chopped cabbage.

Spoon a little of the mixture on to each of the cabbage leaves. Fold in the sides and roll up to make a parcel, then secure it with fine string or thread.

Heat half the oil and butter in a pan and fry the parcels to seal them on all sides. Remove from the pan and set aside. Using the remaining oil and butter, fry the onion until transparent, then add the sieved tomatoes and the paste. Stir and cook for about 15 minutes until thick and enriched, adding a little stock if necessary.

Lay the fried parcels in the sauce and cover. Cook slowly for 1 hour, adding stock if the sauce starts to dry out. Remove the string before serving piping hot.

# POMODORI RIPIENI ALL'UMBRA

## STUFFED TOMATOES IN THE UMBRIAN STYLE

To make this dish successfully you need large, red, round tomatoes that are just a little too soft to be used in salad. It's a deliciously simple recipe from Umbria which can be served as an antipasto to accompany a roast, or as part of an all-vegetable meal with an aubergine dish, a pepper dish and perhaps a courgette or bean dish.

### SERVES 4

*4 huge ripe round tomatoes or 8 smaller ones*
*salt and pepper*
*½ teaspoon tomato paste*
*2 handfuls of fresh white breadcrumbs*
*a handful of fresh parsley, chopped*
*2 cloves garlic, finely chopped*
*3 tablespoons olive oil*
*2 eggs, beaten*
*oil for greasing*

Wash the tomatoes and cut them in half horizontally. Scoop out the inside pulp with great care and sprinkle the inside of the tomatoes with salt. Turn them upside down on the draining board.

Mix the breadcrumbs with plenty of salt, pepper, the tomato paste, parsley, garlic, oil and eggs, then spoon this mixture into the tomatoes. Arrange them in a greased ovenproof dish and bake in a hot oven (200°C, 400°F, gas mark 6) for about 15 minutes. Serve at once.

# POMODORI A RAGANATI

## GRILLED TOMATOES

The cooking term 'a raganati' comes from Apulia and means the same as 'au gratin', but coated in breadcrumbs and then baked in the oven until golden.

SERVES 4

*4 large ripe beefsteak or Marmande tomatoes*
*a large handful of fresh parsley*
*a small handful of fresh basil*
*a very small handful of fresh mint*
*4 tablespoons grated pecorino or Parmesan cheese*
*⅛ teaspoon tomato paste*
*4 tablespoons fresh white breadcrumbs*
*salt and pepper*
*olive oil*

Wash the tomatoes and cut them in half horizontally. Wash and dry the herbs, chop them finely together and mix with the grated cheese, tomato paste and breadcrumbs. Use more cheese than bread if the cheese is not very strongly flavoured, less if it's very mature. Season to taste with salt and pepper.

Remove the seeds from the tomatoes. Arrange the 8 halves in an oiled ovenproof dish. Fill and coat each half with the mixture of herbs, breadcrumbs and cheese. Sprinkle with a little oil and bake in a hot oven (200°C, 400°F, gas mark 6) for 15 minutes. Serve the grilled tomatoes cold, hot or just tepid.

# PEPERONI IMBOTTITI

## STUFFED PEPPERS

The success of this wonderful Campanian speciality depends upon the sweetness and juicy texture of the peppers in the summertime. They must be red and yellow and carefully singed over a naked flame to remove all the outer transparent skin.

An alternative to this filling can be made with small pasta shapes boiled until soft, then dressed with olive oil, capers, chopped anchovies and olives.

SERVES 4

*4 juicy fat red and yellow peppers*
*olive oil*
*115 g (4 oz) cubes of white, slightly stale bread*
*30 g (1 oz) anchovy fillets, cut into thinner strips*
*30 g (1 oz) black olives, stoned and chopped*
*1 teaspoon capers, washed and chopped*
*1 large clove garlic, finely chopped*
*a pinch of dried oregano*
*salt and pepper*

Spear each pepper onto a long-handled fork and hold them, one at a time, over a naked flame, turning the fork so that the pepper blisters all over and goes black. Rub off the outer skin carefully with your fingers, taking care not to split the flesh.

Cut off the end without the stalk and very carefully remove the seeds and membranes from inside the pepper.

Heat enough oil in a frying pan to almost deep fry the bread cubes and fry until golden. Remove with a slotted spoon and drain on kitchen paper. Mix the fried bread with the strips of anchovy, the olives, capers, garlic, oregano and chopped pepper ends. Season well.

Spoon the filling into the peppers, then arrange them, upright, sitting on the stalk in an oiled ovenproof dish. Drizzle a little oil over them and warm them through in a low oven (120°C, 250°F, gas 1) to let the flavours blend for 15 minutes. Serve hot or cold.

*(p 112)* SPINACI ALLA ROMANA *left (p 108)* PANZANELLA *right (p 115)*

# PANZANELLA

## BREAD AND TOMATO SALAD

This is a perfect dish for a summer holiday: it can be made in advance, requires no cooking and is both filling and delicious. My mother can remember her childhood in Tuscany when the sea was so unpolluted that the bread was dipped in the sea, wrapped in a clean cloth, to soak it through. Sadly, this is inadvisable in this day and age.

SERVES 4

*8 thick slices coarse country-style bread*
*5 large ripe firm tomatoes*
*1 cucumber*
*1 large onion*
*8 fresh basil leaves*
*6 tablespoons olive oil*
*2 tablespoons wine vinegar*
*salt and pepper*

Cover the bread in cold water and leave it to soak for about 5 minutes. Squeeze the bread dry in your hands, then put it in a salad bowl.

Slice the tomatoes, cucumber and onion finely, then mix into the bread. Tear the basil into tiny pieces and mix it in also. Dress with the olive oil and vinegar (more olive oil and vinegar can be used if you like a richer dish), season with salt and plenty of pepper and keep in a cool place until required — it is best if left for at least 2 hours.

# MAPPINA

## CHRISTMAS SALAD

This salad is a Calabrian speciality — part of the Christmas scene in the city of Cosenza. It's certainly very unusual, definitely not heavy and the chilli will aid your digestion.

BEAN-PICKING NEAR LIVORNO *In Tuscany the beans are ready for harvesting in July: some will be eaten fresh in salad and stews, the remainder dried and saved for the winter months.*

SERVES 8

*2 endives, escaroles or frisée (which is a chicory), or a mixture, as white and curly as possible*
*4 tablespoons olive oil*
*3 cloves garlic, chopped*
*1 sweet chilli and 2 dried hot chillies, seeded and chopped*
*salt*

Wash and drain the leaves, dry very carefully and chop coarsely. Mix the leaves in a wide bowl, sprinkle with olive oil and scatter chopped garlic, chilli and salt all over it. Put a plate on top and a weight on top of the plate. Leave in a cool place to rest for 2–3 days before eating it.

# MELANZANE A MANNELLA

## AUBERGINE SALAD

This is a wonderful antipasto, an aubergine salad flavoured with garlic and vinegar. Success depends upon the frying — the aubergines must not be greasy.

SERVES 8

*4 large aubergines*
*salt and pepper*
*oil for deep frying*
*3 tablespoons wine vinegar*
*3 cloves garlic, chopped*
*a large pinch of dried oregano*

Slice the aubergines lengthways and arrange them in a wide colander. Scatter over plenty of salt and put a plate on top. Place a heavy weight on the plate and leave them for 1 hour to drain out all their bitter juices.

Heat the oil in a deep-fat fryer to 195°C (385°F). Meanwhile, drain, wash and dry the aubergine slices. Fry them quickly in the oil until crisp and golden, then drain on kitchen paper and cool.

When they are cold, arrange one layer in an ovenproof dish. Scatter with vinegar, oregano and all the garlic and season well. Cover with more aubergines and this time add vinegar and oregano. Place a lid or aluminium foil on the dish and bake in a hot oven (180°C, 350°F, gas mark 4) for 20 minutes. Serve tepid or cold.

# ZUCCA FRITTA

## FRIED PUMPKIN

Pumpkin is very popular all over Lombardy, especially in the areas near Mantua which have been famous for their pumpkin dishes since the times of the Gonzaga court in the 16th century.

SERVES 4

*570 g (1¼ lb) yellow pumpkin*
*milk*
*115 g (4 oz) butter*
*plain flour*
*dried breadcrumbs*
*2 eggs, beaten*

Remove all the seeds from the pumpkin and slice it thickly, removing the skin. Place the slices in a pan, cover with milk, bring to the boil and simmer until soft, but not breaking up. Drain and set aside to cool.

Put the butter in a large pan and begin to melt it slowly. Cover a flat plate with plain flour, and another plate with breadcrumbs and put the beaten eggs in shallow bowl. Dip the cold pumpkin in the flour on both sides, then into the beaten egg, then into the breadcrumbs.

Fry in the hot butter over high heat until crisp and golden on both sides. Add more butter if required. Drain the fried pumpkin on kitchen paper and serve piping hot.

# FRITTO DI FIORI DI ZUCCA

## FRIED COURGETTE FLOWERS

If you grow courgettes or marrows you know how many flowers you get in relation to the number of vegetables! This is a marvellous way of using up all these lovely flowers in a dish which is light and satisfying. Sometimes the flowers tend to be bitter, so it is always best to soak them in some lemon-flavoured water for about 30 minutes, then drain and dry them very carefully.

SERVES 4

*25 courgette or marrow flowers with stalks and pistils*
*lemon juice*
*2 tablespoons plain flour*
*150 ml (5 fl oz) cold milk*
*fine salt*
*1 egg, separated*
*oil for deep frying*

Soak the flowers in lemon-flavoured water for 30 minutes, then gently shake out all the excess water and dry them very gently. Remove the stalks and pistils carefully and set the flowers aside on kitchen paper to finish drying.

Mix the flour into the milk and add a little salt. Beat the egg yolk into the flour and milk mixture. Beat the egg white until stiff, then fold it into the mixture.

Heat the oil in a deep-fat fryer to 195°C (385°F). Dip each flower into the batter, then fry in the oil until puffed and golden brown rolling them over with a slotted spoon. You should be able to fry in batches of 5 or 6. Drain on kitchen paper and sprinkle with salt. Serve hot.

PISELLI IN BARDINO *left (p 102)* ZUCCA FRITTA *right*

# SEDANI CROGIOLATI

## CELERIAC TOASTS

Celeriac stewed in a deliciously smooth sauce, with generous amounts of butter, is served on slices of toasted country bread in this splendid dish from Piedmont. Turnip also works very well in this recipe, but celeriac has such a lovely flavour and texture, it's best to use it provided everybody likes it. Try replacing a quarter of the stock with white wine and adding a couple of teaspoons of tomato paste. It's a dish worth repeating and would make a good opening course, or a vegetarian supper.

### SERVES 4

*3 smallish celeriacs, about 350 g (12 oz) each*
*1 small onion, very finely sliced*
*115 g (4 oz) butter*
*1 tablespoon plain flour*
*225 ml (10 fl oz) good stock*
*salt and pepper*
*4 thick slices country-style bread*
*chopped parsley*

Peel and wash the celeriacs, slice them into rounds, about 5 mm ($\frac{1}{4}$ inch) thick. If using larger celeriac, halve or quarter the rounds. Bring a large pan of water to the boil and add the sliced vegetable. Lower the heat and cook for about 20 minutes.

Meanwhile, fry the onion in the butter until soft. Add the flour and mix it in, cooking it briefly. Add the stock and stir thoroughly.

As soon as the sauce begins to boil and thicken, add the celeriac and season with salt and plenty of pepper. Stir and simmer for 5 minutes. Brown the bread in the oven (or toast it) and then arrange it on a platter. Pour the celeriac and the sauce all over the toast and serve at once with a little parsley on top.

VINES IN PIEDMONT *The vines flourish in the pure air of this mountainous region of Italy.*

118

# ZUCCHINE AL GUANCIALE

## COURGETTES WITH BACON

This dish comes from the Marche region and is traditionally made with guanciale, a local speciality, made from the pig's cheek. It is cured in just the same way as pancetta, which is the usual substitute. It has plenty of lean meat inside the fat, so smoked back bacon or possibly cubed gammon could be used. The courgettes must be young, fresh and tender for the best effect.

SERVES 4

*12 small courgettes*
*salt*
*200 g (7 oz) pancetta or smoked back bacon,*
*cut into strips*
*1 large onion, finely sliced*
*50 g (1¾ oz) chopped fresh parsley*
*2 cloves garlic, chopped*
*4 tablespoons olive oil*
*450 g (1 lb) canned tomatoes, seeded and chopped*
*pepper*

Scrape all the green off the courgettes and slice them lengthways into strips the size of a small finger. Put them on a deep plate and cover with salt to draw out their juices. Leave for about 3 hours.

Fry the bacon, onion, parsley and garlic together in the oil until the onion is soft. Very ripe canned tomatoes don't contain many seeds. Just scoop out any you can see, while adding them and their juice to the pan. Give it a stir and continue to cook.

Wash and dry the courgettes and add to the pan. Stir and simmer for 20 minutes then season with a little salt and plenty of pepper. Give a final stir before serving.

Uova
e
Formaggio

# EGGS AND CHEESE

*The Italian-style omelette is called a frittata, and there are infinite delicious variations; the vast range of cheeses in Italy is a source of national pride and some extremely tasty recipes.*

PIZZA AL FORMAGGIO *left (p 132)*
FRITTATA ROGNOSA *right (p 123)*

A N OMELETTE IN ITALY is always flat and thick, with the filling mixed into the egg mixture or dispersed through it, rather than folded inside it. All these recipes for frittata are prepared in this way, and most of them can be served hot or cold. Often a cold omelette is sliced and sandwiched inside fresh crisp rolls to take on a picnic. I like to serve a frittata as a first course — especially an onion or artichoke frittata; or a whole selection of them with different flavourings and fillings — as long as my hens cooperate and start producing 19 eggs per day between them! Apart from the truffle frittatas, all the others are very cheap and basic, using ingredients which are readily at hand. You can vary the thickness and size of your omelette once you have mastered the turning over process. And if you have difficulty with them sticking at first, just put the pan under the grill to set the top.

Always choose the best quality free-range eggs for these recipes, and if you have to use the battery variety, make sure they are cooked for at least six minutes.

As far as cheese goes, if Parmesan is king of Italian cheeses (with grana Padano in shadowy attendance) then the queen of Italian cheeses has to be mozzarella — the best variety being Mozzarella di Buffala, made with rich buffalo milk. Ricotta is another very important cheese, which features particularly in dessert and cake making. The Italians are as fussy and concerned about their vast range of cheeses as the French, and as more people discover the versatility and variety of Italian cheeses, one begins to see just why this is so. A particular favourite of mine is Caprino, a sausage-shaped creamy-white goat's cheese which is delicious with a dressing of olive oil, salt and masses of freshly ground black pepper.

Another deliciously simple cheese dish is a sliver of Parmesan or grana laid out flat on a platter and sprinkled with lemon juice, olive oil, chopped parsley and slices of raw mushroom. I am especially fond of the recipes in this section, but there are so many others — melted gorgonzola with polenta, which I have already mentioned, then gorgonzola and cream tossed with spaghetti, the superb cheese fondues of the northern regions, and the fantastic salad of tomatoes and mozzarella, which originally comes from the island of Capri and must have lots of fresh basil to complete it.

I think most of these recipes are perfect for simple suppers or as first courses, and the truffle frittatas are always a great success at dinner parties as a way of serving truffles which sets off their distinctive flavour.

# FRITTATA ROGNOSA

## SALAMI AND CHEESE OMELETTE

In Piedmont, when they make this omelette they use a special kind of salami which is kept soft in terracotta pots; any other kind of Italian salami will do provided it isn't too hard and chewy. If you buy sausages with skins, take them off before cubing them.

### SERVES 4

*115 g (4 oz) good soft salami, chopped into squares*
*5 eggs*
*8 tablespoons freshly grated Parmesan cheese*
*salt and pepper*

Fry the salami in a heavy omelette pan until all the fat is running. Beat the eggs with the cheese and a pinch each of salt and pepper. When the salami fat is sizzling in the pan, tip in the egg mixture and cook the omelette over high heat until the underneath is crisp and golden.

Turn it out on to a large plate or lid, then slide it back into the pan the other way up and cook until the other side is golden. Serve hot with salad and bread.

# OMELETTA DI PATATE CRUDE

## POTATO OMELETTE

Italians have distinctly different ideas about omelettes from the French. The Italian frittata is generally cooked through, and is not the creamy-centred, almost runny affair which the French fold round a filling. The frittata is definitely flat and usually includes a number of flavouring extras, which must be cooked in the pan before the eggs are added.

In Italy potatoes are given as much attention as other vegetables like peppers and mushrooms. This is a basic and delicious standby – almost everyone usually has potatoes and eggs in the house. In poor peasant households this would constitute a good nourishing lunch, especially when accompanied by some fresh green vegetables or a refreshing salad.

### SERVES 4

*1 strip pork belly or 2 rashers bacon, chopped*
*into small cubes*
*2–3 tablespoons oil or dripping*
*4 small potatoes, unpeeled but cubed*
*1 small onion, sliced*
*5 eggs, beaten*
*salt and pepper*

In a heavy omelette pan, fry the pork belly or bacon with 2 tablespoons oil or dripping until they give off their fat. Add the potatoes and onions and fry over low heat, until the onions are softened, turning the potatoes often to cook them through. If any of the ingredients start to get too crisp, add a little water and scrape to loosen, and then another spoonful of oil.

When the potatoes are cooked through, turn up the heat a little, pour in the eggs and season with salt and pepper. Cook until the omelette is crisp and golden underneath. Turn it out on to a plate or lid, then slide it back into the pan the other way up and cook until the other side is also golden. Serve piping hot.

# FRITTATA ALLA BARCAROLA

## BOATMAN'S OMELETTE

This is a speciality of the Ligurian Riviera and eating it is sure to bring back the memories of that area with its sparkling light and brilliant flowers. Use salted anchovies if you can possibly get hold of them, as they give the best result for this omelette.

SERVES 2

*5 eggs*
*1 clove garlic, finely chopped*
*a handful of fresh parsley, finely chopped*
*3 salted anchovies, washed or 6 anchovy fillets in oil*
*about 3 tablespoons olive oil*
*3 fresh ripe tomatoes, peeled, seeded and chopped*
*¼ teaspoon tomato paste (if needed)*
*salt and pepper*

Beat the eggs thoroughly in a bowl. Fry the garlic, parsley and anchovies in 1 tablespoon of the olive oil. Remove all the bones from anchovies bought from a barrel. If you are using canned fillets, drain but don't bother to blot them. Cook until the anchovy has disintegrated and the garlic is soft and mushy.

Add the tomatoes and the tomato paste too, if they don't look ripe enough. Season with pepper but little salt, bearing in mind that the anchovies are already quite salty. Mix well, then simmer for about 5–6 minutes, then tip the mixture into the eggs. Mix together and set aside.

Heat about 2 tablespoons of oil in a heavy omelette pan, pour in the egg mixture and cook the omelette over medium heat until the underneath is crisp and golden. Turn it out on to a large plate or lid and slide it back into the pan the other way up and cook until the other side is golden. Drain on kitchen paper to remove excess oil, then serve hot or cold. This makes a main course for two or an attractive starter for four with salad.

# FRITTATA DI CIPOLLE

## ONION OMELETTE

This delicious flat omelette from Campania has a hint of mint as well as the traditional flavours of tomato and basil. It tastes best served cold and is a perfect dish to take on a picnic, as it is solid but very tasty. If you are not too keen on eating fat, you can halve the quantity of pork fat.

SERVES 4

*olive oil*
*115 g (4 oz) pork fat, chopped*
*75 g (2½ oz) prosciutto crudo, in one thick slice, chopped*
*800 g (1 lb 10 oz) large onions, sliced*
*6 fresh mint leaves, chopped or a pinch of dried mint*
*8 eggs*
*3 tablespoons freshly grated Parmesan cheese*
*2 tablespoons grated pecorino cheese*
*a handful of fresh basil, chopped or*
*1 tablespoon dried basil*
*4 ripe tomatoes, peeled and seeded*
*salt and pepper*

Put 1 tablespoon of oil and the pork fat in a heavy omelette pan and cook until the fat is almost melted and crisp. Then add the prosciutto, onions and mint, and cook slowly until the onions are soft. Beat the eggs in a bowl, then stir in the grated cheeses and basil.

Cut the tomatoes into strips and cook them in a little oil for 5 minutes. As soon as the onions are cooked through and the tomatoes soft, tip both into the egg mixture, season with salt and pepper and mix it all together very thoroughly.

Heat about 6 tablespoons of oil in a heavy omelette pan and when it is sizzling, tip in the egg mixture. Cook the omelette over low heat until the underneath is crisp and golden, then turn it out on to a plate or lid and slide it back into the pan the other way up. Cook until the other side is golden, then slide it out on to a plate and leave it to cool before serving.

OLIVE TREES WITH LAVENDER *Fragrant clumps of lavender keep the ground free of weeds around these healthy olive trees.*

# FRITTATA DI TARTUFI

## UMBRIAN BLACK TRUFFLE OMELETTE

In Umbria the locals use the delectable black truffle rather like the rest of us use parsley – in generous quantities with not a lot of regard for its value on the market! In sizeable chunks, it flavours this rustic omelette to make it something really special. The important thing is that the truffles should be absolutely fresh and that they should not stew as the eggs cook, so make sure the omelette stays soft and slightly runny in the centre. If truffles are out of the question, flavour the omelette with truffle paste to taste. A friend tried this for me with a small tube and suggested beating the eggs first and then stirring in the truffle paste, so that it does not break up too much. This gives the omelette a more interesting colour and texture, rather than an overall grey.

SERVES 2—4

*115 g (4 oz) black truffles*
*5 eggs*
*salt and pepper*
*5 tablespoons cream*
*30 g (1 oz) butter*
*juice of ½ a lemon*

Brush the truffles, wipe them with warm water and a cloth and then grate them or cut them into chunks. Beat the eggs with a little salt and pepper and the cream, then add the truffles.

Heat the butter in a heavy omelette pan until melted and hot but not sizzling or changing colour. Tip in the egg and truffle mixture. Cook over low heat until golden on the underside. Then turn the omelette out on to a plate or lid, slide back into the pan the other way up. Cook until the other side is golden, bearing in mind that the centre of the omelette should stay soft and runny. Cut it into little slices and sprinkle with lemon juice just before serving.

**SARDINIAN CHEESES ON A BALCONY** *Small-scale manufacture is what makes real Italian food so delicious – here eight rounds of fresh cheese ripen under the Sardinian sun.*

# UOVA ALLA PIEMONTESE

## EGGS COOKED IN THE PIEDMONT STYLE

The white truffle grows happily in the mountainous woods of Piedmont, where seeking them out is very big business indeed. Once there must have been a time when it was a simple natural food resource like berries and wild mushrooms. In the area around Alba, it is especially popular and many families spend happy hours with their

dogs seeking out the tubers for household use. They are always used simply. If you cannot find a fresh truffle, make the black truffle recipe instead.

SERVES 4

*5 eggs*
*1 white truffle*
*a handful of freshly grated Parmesan cheese*
*salt and pepper*
*30 g (1 oz) butter*
*1 tablespoon olive oil*

Beat the eggs, then grate the truffle in incredibly thin slices into the bowl using a truffle or cheese grater – it should almost be shaved! Add cheese and salt and pepper and beat again.

Heat the butter and oil in a heavy omelette pan until sizzling, then pour in the egg mixture. Cook the omelette until the underneath is crisp and golden. Turn the egg and truffle mixture out on to a plate or lid. Slide it back into the pan the other way up and cook until golden on the other side, making sure that the centre of the omelette stays slightly runny. Serve hot or cold.

# FRITTATA CON FIORI DI ZUCCA

## OMELETTE WITH COURGETTE FLOWERS

In peasant cooking, nothing is ever wasted and the flowers of the courgette plant are deliciously sweet and tasty.

SERVES 4

*400 g (13 oz) courgette flowers with stalks and pistils*
*lemon juice*
*plain flour*
*olive oil*
*4 eggs, beaten*
*salt and pepper*

Soak the flowers in lemon-flavoured water for 30 minutes, then gently shake out all the excess water and dry them very gently. Remove the stalks and pistils carefully and set the flowers aside on kitchen paper to finish drying. Dip the flowers in flour.

Pour enough oil into a heavy omelette pan to come to a depth of about 4 cm (1½ inches) and heat until sizzling. Add the flowers in batches and fry until golden and crisp on all sides. Spoon out most of the oil and return all the flowers to the pan.

Season the beaten eggs, with salt and pepper, then pour them over all the flowers. Cook the omelette until the underneath is golden. Turn it out on to a plate or lid. Slide it back into the pan the other way up and cook until the other side is golden.

# FRITTATA AFFOGATA

## DROWNED OMELETTE

This traditional speciality from the area around the beautiful city of Arezzo is a delicious alternative to a pasta dish. It consists of strips of firm omelette dressed with a tomato sauce and cheese. Served with a crisp salad and plenty of bread to soak up the sauce, it makes a lovely supper or lunch dish.

SERVES 4

*5 eggs*
*1 teaspoon plain flour*
*2 tablespoons dried breadcrumbs*
*salt and pepper*
*olive oil*
*1 onion, finely chopped*
*1 stick celery, finely chopped*
*1 carrot, finely chopped*
*1 clove garlic, finely chopped*
*6 canned tomatoes, seeded and chopped*

Beat the eggs in a bowl with the flour, breadcrumbs and salt and pepper. Heat a little oil in a heavy omelette pan until sizzling, then pour in the egg mixture. Cook until crisp and golden, then turn it out on to a plate or lid and slide it back into the pan the other way up and cook until the other side is golden. Slide it out on to kitchen paper, drain and leave to go completely cold.

Meanwhile, fry the onion, celery and carrot in the omelette pan until the onion is soft, then add the garlic and tomatoes. Season with salt and pepper, mix well and simmer until you have a smooth rich sauce, about 20 minutes. Slice the omelette into strips, add to the tomato sauce and heat through for 5 minutes before serving.

In a heavy omelette pan, fry the bacon in the oil until crisp and all the fat has run out. Italians, like Americans, think perfect bacon consists of well-crisped fat, and not pink lean meat. Beat the eggs with salt and pepper, then pour on top of the bacon.

Cook the omelette over low heat until the underneath is crisp and golden, then turn it out on to a plate or lid and slide it back into the pan the other way up and cook until the other side is golden. Serve at once.

# US IN FONGHET

## EGGS IN A
## TOMATO AND MUSHROOM SAUCE

This is a speciality of the peasant cuisine of Venezia Giulia. It is generally considered not to be the sort of dish to serve to a special guest – which is a shame as the flavour is so delicious, especially when the wild mushroom season is at its peak in the autumn.

### SERVES 8

*8 eggs*
*salt and pepper*
*a handful of fresh parsley, finely chopped*
*1 tablespoon olive oil*
*75 g (2½ oz) butter*
*2 cloves garlic, chopped*
*225 g (8 oz) fresh ceps (or other fresh*
*wild mushrooms), sliced*
*225 g (8 oz) canned tomatoes, seeded and chopped*

Place the eggs in a pan of cold water, bring to the boil and cook for 6 minutes. Remove from the heat, dip in cold water and remove the shells. Cut them in half lengthways, sprinkle with salt and pepper and then with the parsley.

Fry the oil, butter and garlic together for a minute in a wide pan. Add the mushrooms and the tomatoes, stir and cook for 10 minutes. Arrange the eggs, cut side up, in the sauce. Add a little water and cook over a very low heat for a further 10 minutes, spooning the sauce over the eggs from time to time. Serve hot as a starter or with fried slices of polenta (page 54) as a main course.

BACKSTREET SHOP *(p 129) This shop advertises the four essentials for the Italian cook – olive oil, grana cheese, prosciutto and wine.*

CYPRESS TREES *(p 128) This farmer has made an avenue of cypress trees dividing his meadow from the ploughed land.*

# FRITTATA CON GLI ZOCCOLI

## BACON OMELETTE

This bacon omelette is a typical Tuscan country dish. It is perfection when accompanied by a radicchio salad.

### SERVES 4

*115 g (4 oz) smoked streaky bacon,*
*cut into little chunks*
*5 tablespoons olive oil*
*5 eggs*
*salt and pepper*

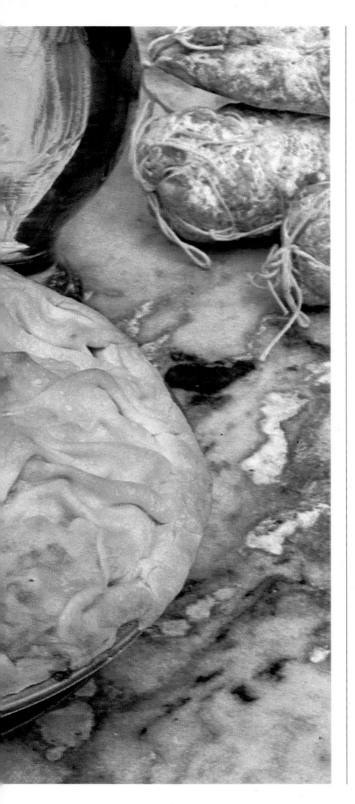

# TORTINO ALLE ERBE

## SAVOURY SPINACH CAKE

In Emilia Romagna they are very keen on savoury cakes, such as this one which is a flattish cake-shaped 'pie', cut into slices and serve from the tin.

### SERVES 6–8

*1.2 kg (2½ lb) spinach or tender Swiss chard, washed and stalks trimmed off*
*salt*
*120 ml (4 fl oz) olive oil, plus extra for drizzling*
*a handful of fresh basil, chopped*
*225 g (8 oz) freshly grated Parmesan cheese (or half Parmesan and half pecorino cheese)*
*150 g (5 oz) plain flour*
*1 tablespoon lard*

Cut the spinach or chard into strips. Sprinkle it liberally with salt in a wide bowl, turning it over with your hands so that it all gets covered with salt.

Leave it to rest for 1 hour, then squeeze out all the water with your hands, dry it carefully and put it back into the dried bowl. Add the oil, basil and cheese and mix it all together. Set aside.

Put the flour, lard and about 4 tablespoons cold water in a bowl and knead to a fairly stiff dough. Grease a 25 cm (10 inch) cake tin with a little oil. Divide the dough into 2 pieces, one slightly larger than the other.

Roll out the larger piece of dough and line the cake tin with it. Put the spinach or chard filling inside, smoothing it so that it is level. Roll out the second piece of dough until it is really thin, then place it on top of the tin like a tablecloth – the art of this dish is in the draping! Great contests have arisen between cooks and housewives as to who could make the draped dough look most decorative.

Pinch the edges together all the way around the circle, pushing the extra flap of dough back on to the surface of the cake. Prick tiny holes in the surface to allow the steam to escape and paint a little olive oil all over the cake to make it crisp. Bake in a moderate oven (180°C, 350°F, gas mark 4) for 1 hour. Drizzle fresh olive oil all over it before serving it piping hot, cut into slices.

TORTINO ALLE ERBE

# PANDORATO

## GOLDEN BREAD

This is a speciality from the countryside towns of the Lazio, the province around Rome. Like all the cuisine of this area, it is a fairly heavy dish with a good substantial texture. Serve as an antipasto or as a lunchtime snack (if they are prepared in advance) with plenty of fresh green salad. Also an ideal picnic food.

### SERVES 4

*400 g (13 oz) thick sliced white bread*
*100 g (3½ oz) prosciutto crudo, in slices*
*2 small or 1 large mozzarella cheese, sliced*
*250 ml (8 fl oz) milk*
*salt*
*2 large eggs, beaten*
*oil for deep frying (or half oil and half lard)*

Cut all the crusts off the bread and cut each slice in half to make a rectangle. Cut the prosciutto to the same size. Make sandwiches, putting a slice of prosciutto and mozzarella cheese in each one. Use more prosciutto and mozzarella than bread if you get towards the end and still have some left.

Dip the sandwiches in milk (dip not soak), then arrange all the sandwiches on a large platter. Add a little salt to the eggs, then pour them over the sandwiches. Leave to soak for 2 hours.

Heat the oil in a deep-fat fryer to 195°C (385°F). Fry the egg-soaked sandwiches in a basket, a few at a time, until crisp and golden on both sides. Remove them and drain on kitchen paper. Serve very hot.

# PIZZA AL FORMAGGIO

## CHEESE LOAF

This is the essential companion for Verdicchio wine, and both are specialities of the lovely medieval town of Iesi in the Marche region. It is baked in a type of tall cake tin that foreigners associate more with Austria and Eastern Europe than with Italy. Empty preserving cans may be used as a substitute.

### MAKES 2 × 450 g (1 lb) LOAVES

*20 g (¾ oz) fresh yeast, diluted in a little warm water*
*340 g (12 oz) plain white flour*
*1½ teaspoons salt*
*1 tablespoon olive oil plus extra for greasing the tin*
*55 g (2 oz) Gruyère cheese, grated*
*55 g (2 oz) Parmesan cheese, grated*
*55 g (2 oz) provolone cheese, grated*
*2 eggs beaten*
*30 g (1 oz) Gruyère cheese, cubed*
*30 g (1 oz) Parmesan cheese, cubed or flaked*
*30 g (1 oz) provolone cheese, cubed*
*30 g (1 oz) pecorino or Parmesan cheese, cubed*

Mix together 100 g (3½ oz) of the flour, the yeast and a pinch of salt. Knead together, adding 150 ml (5 fl oz) tepid water — just enough to make an elastic dough. Cover and leave in a warm place to rise.

Mix the remaining flour with the oil and a pinch of salt. Knead carefully adding about 75 ml (2½ fl oz) tepid water, enough to make a dough that is soft, elastic and even.

Put all the grated cheese in a bowl and mix together. Add the beaten eggs and mix, then add all the cubed cheese. Add the second lot of dough (the one without yeast) and mix together.

Turn the cheese dough out on to the work top and add the risen dough to it. Knead and mix together until well combined.

In Italy we have tall, narrow cake tins, but you will probably have to bake in two empty 450 g (1 lb) cans. Oil them and place the kneaded ball of dough in each can. Cover with a clean cloth and leave to rise again for 45 minutes. Bake in a hot oven (200°C, 400°F, gas mark 6) for 30–40 minutes. Serve hot.

# CICORIA, UOVA E CACIO

## CHICORY, EGGS AND CHEESE

The most delicious of all the winter warmers from the chilly Abruzzi winters. White chicory can be used if the heads are cooked first for 15 minutes.

### SERVES 4

*450 g (1 lb) wild chicory or endive, or sorrel very carefully cleaned and washed*
*salt*
*1.2 litres (2 pints) chicken or beef broth*
*2 carrots, scraped and finely chopped*
*3 onions, finely chopped*
*1 stick celery, chopped*

ABRUZZI MARKET *An open market showing a cheese stall. The very dark cheeses are the ones matured for grating.*

*5 sprigs of fresh parsley*
*55 g (2 oz) pork fat, chopped*
*2 large eggs*
*75 g (2¼ oz) pecorino or Parmesan cheese, grated*

Blanch the leaves in plenty of boiling salted water. Drain then leave it to soak in cold water for 2 hours.

Bring the broth to the boil with the carrots, 2 of the onions, the celery and parsley, simmer until they are cooked. Fry the pork fat with the remaining onion.

Drain the leaves and squeeze them out between your hands to get rid of all the water. Chop and add to the pan.

Turn and mix it very carefully. Bring the broth back to the boil. Beat the eggs with the pecorino in the bottom of the soup tureen. Add the leaves and mix it all together. Pour the broth on top, mix once more and serve.

# FORMAGGIO FRITTO

## FRIED CHEESE

It is important to use a really mature cheese for this peasant dish from Friuli – any kind of stracchino will do, as long as it isn't crumbly.

### SERVES 4

*300 g (10 oz) mature cheese such as taleggio or a creamy gorgonzola, cut into even slices*
*5 tablespoons polenta (yellow cornmeal)*
*115 g (4 oz) unsalted butter*
*4 eggs*
*salt and pepper*

Dip the cheese into the polenta to coat it lightly on both sides. The grains of the flour are quite sharp and will embed themselves easily into the soft cheese surface.

Put about two-thirds of the butter into a frying pan and heat until bubbling hot. Place the cheese slices in the butter and fry them thoroughly on both sides.

In a separate pan, heat the remaining butter and fry the eggs. Serve the cheese and the eggs piping hot seasoned with salt and pepper, with bread as a starter or snack.

# MOZZARELLA IMPANATA

## FRIED MOZZARELLA

Down in Campania they love mozzarella only slightly less than they love tomatoes and there are many recipes for using it in different ways. Traditionally the cheese is made from buffalo milk, from animals first introduced in the 16th century. But even in Italy this is becoming rarer. The egg-shaped mozzarella are packed in their own whey, to keep them moist, and are sold in sealed packs in two basic sizes. It is a much-loved cheese for cooking because of the way it binds ingredients together when it melts. In this recipe it makes a delicious melted filling inside a crisp, flavoured crust.

### SERVES 4

*2 eggs*
*salt and pepper*
*plain flour*
*115 g (4 oz) stale breadcrumbs*
*a pinch of dried oregano*
*2 small or 1 large mozzarella cheese*
*oil for deep frying*

Beat the eggs in a soup plate with a little salt. Spread out the flour and breadcrumbs on separate plates. Salt and pepper the crumbs generously and sprinkle with oregano. Cut the mozzarella into slices 2 cm (¾ inch) thick.

Dip the mozzarella slices into the flour, then into the egg, then into the breadcrumbs. Heat the oil in a deep-fat fryer to 195°C (385°F). Deep fry about 4 slices at a time in a basket for 2–3 minutes, then remove and drain on kitchen paper. When they are all ready, serve at once.

### SERVES 4

*4 salted anchovies or 8 anchovy fillets in oil*
*8 slices thick white bread*
*100 g (3½ oz) unsalted butter*
*3 canned tomatoes, seeded and cut into strips*
*2 small or 1 large mozzarella cheese, sliced*
*salt and pepper*
*a pinch of dried oregano*
*oil for greasing*

Wash the anchovies, de-scale them and cut them in half lengthways, then cut each length in half again to make 16 strips. Alternatively, blot anchovy fillets with kitchen paper and split them lengthways.

Cut the bread slices in half and spread one side thickly with butter. Then place a piece of tomato, a piece of mozzarella cheese and a piece of anchovy on each slice. Season with salt and pepper and a generous pinch of oregano.

Grease an oven tray, place the bread slices on it and bake in a moderate oven (180°C, 350°F, gas mark 4) for 9 minutes before serving.

CROSTINI ALLA NAPOLETANA *(p 134)*

# CROSTINI ALLA NAPOLETANA

## NEAPOLITAN ANTIPASTO

To get the real flavour of this popular antipasto dish you will need to try and get hold of proper salted anchovies. If you can't find them, use the ones preserved in oil.

# SWEET THINGS

*Sweet treats for Carnival and the festive season, subtle, spiced puddings and delicious dunking biscuits: Italy's traditional sweets will delight children and grown-ups alike and remain as popular today as ever.*

GESMINUS *left (p 154)* GELATO DI COCOMERO *centre (p 155)* TARALLI *right (p 154)*

MOST OF THE RECIPES throughout this book were originally designed for feeding a family on what little there was available. With that sort of ideal, the sweet course must be viewed very much as a treat. In fact, quite a few of these recipes are for the kind of cake and biscuit which would be dunked into coffee at breakfast time, or eaten as a snack at teatime rather than as a dessert at the end of the meal. The ingredients are all fairly basic and cheap, the antithesis of the impressive, flambée dessert carried to the table with a flourish. Prepared mostly with the children in mind, a few of them are treats prepared for Carnival-time, Christmas, or weddings and other such occasions, or for times of plenty when there was an abundance of sugar, eggs and flour available.

There are a lot of fried sweet things, such as fritters, because they are simple, nourishing and traditionally very popular – especially at Carnival. Please, please remember to put the hot oil out of everybody's way when you have finished frying, so that it cannot be reached by small or big hands! It is also important to remember that when frying in large batches, the temperature must be kept constant so it is vital to continually adjust the heat under the pan containing the fat. Do not allow the fat to simply get hotter and hotter as you fry, because you will find the food becoming a less and less desirable shade of burnt – and there is, of course the added danger of fire.

Cakes are very much a breakfast food, delicious with foaming, milky coffee or hot chocolate. 'Teatime' does not exist as a meal, but 'merenda' is the nearest equivalent – an afternoon snack for children in between their lunch and supper – this could be a slice of cake or a doughnut or maybe fritters of some sort. I can remember taking slices of Castagnaccio (chestnut flour cake) to school with me to eat at mid-morning break. I have always loved it, but it is not to everyone's taste – it may surprise and outrage aficionados, but many people actually don't like chestnuts. The alternative to Castagnaccio is to make the same dough and then fry it into little pancakes which must be sandwiched while still very hot on either side of a slab of stracchino cheese so that it begins to melt.

There is a wider variety of sweet things in Sicily than anywhere else in the country, though for the most part they are extremely rich and filled with various ingredients which do not necessarily marry particularly well. In the north also they tend to go quite mad with their variety of sweet things – using masses of whipped cream and delectable chocolate. But the sweets I have chosen are very simple and basic, following the character of the other recipes. My favourite is the delicious rice-cake on page 141, which I consider special enough for dessert at the end of a dinner party.

The further south one goes, the more honey enters the scene as an ingredient in cakes and sweet things generally, an obvious link with the Mediterranean past, when this part of Italy was a domain of Greece – almonds have entered into the cuisine for very much the same reason. Chocolate was only introduced in the latter part of the 16th century and as most of the recipes date back far earlier, it only features twice. Although the recipes are so very old, many are as popular today as they were then.

# CASTAGNACCIO

## CHESTNUT FLOUR CAKE

This must be one of the very oldest of all the cakes eaten in poor Italian households. It is extraordinarily nourishing and full of goodness and used to be a great favourite with schoolchildren, who would take hot thick slices of it wrapped in paper to eat on the way to school. Chestnut flour is available at good Italian delicatessens.

### SERVES 6

*115 g (4 oz) sultanas*
*450 g (1 lb) chestnut flour, sieved*
*½ teaspoon salt*
*cold water*
*olive oil*
*1 tablespoon caraway seeds*
*3 tablespoons pine nuts*
*½ teaspoon dried rosemary*

Cover the sultanas with cold water and leave them to soak for 15 minutes; drain and dry. Mix together the chestnut flour and salt and stir in enough cold water to make a batter which is slightly thicker than pancake batter.

Oil a shallow cake tin and pour in the batter, smooth it with a spoon, then scatter over the caraway seeds, pine nuts, rosemary and sultanas.

Drizzle a little more oil over the top and bake in a moderately hot oven (190°C, 375°F, gas mark 5) for 10–15 minutes or until the surface is crispy. Serve warm or cold with chilled white wine.

# PIZZA DI POLENTA

## POLENTA COUNTRY CAKE

This ancient recipe from the countryside surrounding Rome calls for real Roman ricotta cheese, diluted with water. I have used a mixture of half cream cheese and half cottage cheese very successfully when ricotta has been unavailable. This is a delicious and unusual cake, best when served oven-warm.

### SERVES 6

*30 g (1 oz) sultanas or currants*
*225 g (8 oz) Roman ricotta cheese (see above)*
*225 g (8 oz) granulated sugar*
*225 g (8 oz) polenta (yellow cornmeal)*
*a large pinch of ground cinnamon*
*15 g (1 oz) butter, plus extra for greasing*
*2 tablespoons pine nuts*

Soak the sultanas or currants in water for 15 minutes; drain and dry. Mix the ricotta cheese, with 500 ml (18 fl oz) cold water, whisking with a balloon whisk or fork.

Whisk the sugar into this mixture, then slowly tip in the polenta, stirring constantly. Stir in the cinnamon and the sultanas. Grease a 25 cm (10 inch) loose-bottomed cake tin with butter and pour in the cake mixture. Dot with a few scraps of butter and scatter the pine nuts over the top. Bake in a slow oven (150°C, 300°F, gas mark 2) for 1¾ hours. Serve while still warm.

# CIAMBELLINE CAMPAGNOLE

## COUNTRY RING CAKES

These ring cakes came originally from the Molise but are fairly typical of rustic little cakes all over the country. They are good dipping biscuits for mulled wine.

### MAKES ABOUT 15

*115 g (4 oz) granulated sugar*
*1 glass, 120 ml (4 fl oz), red wine*
*100 ml (3½ fl oz) olive oil*
*about 225 g (8 oz) plain flour*
*lard for greasing*

Mix the sugar and wine together, add the oil and mix in enough flour to make a kneadable dough. Turn it out on to a table and knead until smooth. Put it in a bowl, cover with a cloth and leave to rest for 1–2 hours.

Thoroughly grease a baking sheet. Break pieces off the dough and roll them into little snake shapes, wind them into rings and arrange them on the greased baking tray. Bake in a warm oven (160°C, 325°F, gas mark 3) for 20 minutes. Cool and store until required.

# TORTA DI GRANOTURCO

## CORNMEAL AND NUT CAKE

This is a very basic cake, reputedly the most rustic of all Italian cakes, because it is made with cornmeal, which has no rising properties. Combined with almonds and sugar, it makes a very flat sweet cake. The recipe is from the region of Lombardy, where it is eaten at breakfast time by children on their way to school.

Granoturco, meaning 'Turkish corn', is the Italian name for maize, because the grain first came to them from the East. With the emphasis on sugar and nuts, this is rather an Eastern sweetmeat too.

SERVES 8

*300 g (10 oz) finest possible polenta (cornmeal)*
*300 g (10 oz) caster sugar*
*300 g (10 oz) unsalted butter, melted*
*300 g (10 oz) ground almonds*
*butter for greasing*
*dried breadcrumbs for coating the cake tin*

Sift the flour twice, then sift it twice more with the sugar. Stir in the almonds and melted butter and mix thoroughly. Grease a 25 cm (10 inch) cake tin with butter, then coat completely with the breadcrumbs.

Turn the cake mixture into the tin and bake in a hot oven (200°C, 400°F, gas mark 6) for 40 minutes. Cool in the tin, then turn out.

## TORTA SABBIOSA

### SANDY CAKE

Although this cake comes originally from the Veneto region, it is extremely popular all over the country and is the kind of cake kept in the larder for when friends come to call – it can be served with cold white wine. It is deliciously crumbly, hence its name of 'sandy', and melts in the mouth. But its success depends very much on the correct working of butter and sugar together and in the oven being kept at the correct temperature.

SERVES 8

*320 g (11 oz) unsalted butter*
*300 g (10 oz) caster sugar*
*3 eggs, separated*
*2 tablespoons milk if needed*
*150 g (5 oz) cornflour*
*150 g (5 oz) plain flour*
*¼ teaspoon baking powder*
*a pinch of salt*

Using 20 g (¾ oz) of the butter, grease a 25 cm (10 inch) cake tin. Cream the remaining butter with the sugar until really fluffy and light. Add the yolks one at a time, working each one into the mixture before adding the next. Add milk if needed to make a batter with dropping consistency.

Sift in the cornflour, flour, baking powder and salt, mixing all the time. Whisk the egg whites until stiff, then fold in. Turn into the cake tin and bake in a moderate oven (180°C, 350°F, gas mark 4) for 1¼ hours without ever opening the door of the oven or creating a draught in the kitchen. Leave to cool, then remove it from the cake tin.

HAYMAKING *Oxen pull a cart laden with loose straw through the meadow and home to the farm.*

## TORTA DI RISO

### RICE CAKE

A pure nostalgic 'fix' for me. This cake represents all the best days of my childhood in Tuscany, eaten at no particular time of day and for no particular reason other than 'it is good for you'. Use pudding rice for the right texture – it is not unlike rice pudding.

SERVES 8

*about 900 ml (1½ pints) milk*
*200 g (7 oz) granulated sugar*
*300 g (10 oz) pudding rice*
*3 eggs, beaten*
*1 teaspoon vanilla essence*
*115 g (4 oz) candied peel, chopped*
*50 g (1¾ oz) pine nuts*
*55 g (2 oz) unsalted butter*
*grated rind of ½ a lemon*
*4 walnuts, cracked and chopped*
*50 g (1¾ oz) shelled pistachio nuts, chopped*

Put the milk and the sugar into a pan and bring to the boil. Just as it begins to boil, add the rice, stir and simmer until all the milk has been absorbed – a little more may be needed depending on the variety of rice used. Leave to cool.

When cold, add the eggs, vanilla essence, candied peel, pine nuts, three-quarters of the butter, the lemon rind, walnuts and pistachio nuts. Mix it all together very thoroughly. Use the remaining butter to grease a 28 cm (11 inch) cake tin. Turn the mixture into the tin and bake in a hot oven (200°C, 400°F, gas mark 6) for 30 minutes. Cool, then turn it out on to a serving platter and serve.

# FOCACCIA ALLA CECCOBEPPE

## VENETIAN COUNTRY CAKE

One of the most thrifty and delicious of all the country cakes, this uses up all the leftover bits of stale bread from around the house. It tastes good, even in comparison to modern cakes, and is superb at breakfast time.

### SERVES 12

*about 300 g (10 oz) stale breadcrumbs*
*(as fine as possible)*
*30 g (1 oz) butter*
*30 g (1 oz) sultanas*
*75 g (2¼ oz) assorted candied fruit, finely chopped*
*8 eggs, separated*
*225 g (8 oz) granulated or caster sugar*
*grated rind of 1 lemon*
*a pinch of salt*
*¼ teaspoon lemon juice*
*about 2 tablespoons icing sugar*

Sift the breadcrumbs and measure out 225 g (8 oz). Put these breadcrumbs into a bowl and set aside. Butter a fairly deep cake tin (or ovenproof dish), add the remaining breadcrumbs, turning the tin to coat the bottom and sides with crumbs. Discard any excess crumbs.

Cover the sultanas in cold water and leave to soak for 15 minutes, then drain and dry them. Mix the candied fruit with the sultanas. Put the 8 egg yolks and the sugar into a large mixing bowl and whisk until pale yellow and foamy. Add the reserved breadcrumbs a little at a time, mixing all the time. Stir in the candied fruit and sultanas, then the lemon rind. Add a pinch of salt and stir very carefully.

Whisk the egg whites with the lemon juice until stiff, then fold them into the breadcrumb mixture very carefully. When smooth and evenly mixed, turn it into the prepared tin and bake in a moderate oven (180°C, 350°F, gas mark 4) for 45 minutes. Take it out of the oven and cool for 1 minute, then remove from the tin and sprinkle with the icing sugar. Leave to cool on a serving platter.

# BUDINO DI PATATE

## POTATO PUDDING

A Friulan pudding of Slavic origin, this one is made with potatoes, with sultanas, butter, pine nuts and various spices added. It is delicious, and very light.

SERVES 4−6

*115 g (4 oz) sultanas*
*450 g (1 lb) potatoes, washed but not peeled*
*85 g (3 oz) unsalted butter, plus extra for greasing*
*8 tablespoons single cream, plus extra for serving*
*a pinch of salt*
*1 tablespoon plain flour*
*85 g (3 oz) granulated sugar*
*a pinch of ground cinnamon*

*a pinch of grated nutmeg*
*3 eggs, separated*
*75 g (2½ oz) pine nuts*
*1 tablespoon icing sugar for dusting*

Cover the sultanas with cold water and set aside to plump up. Cover the potatoes with cold water and cook until soft. Peel them and mash in a pan. Add the butter, cream, salt and flour and mix together over low heat. Add the sugar, spices and egg yolks and mix very thoroughly, then turn the mixture into a bowl.

Whisk the egg whites until stiff, then fold them into the mixture. Squeeze out the excess water from the sultanas and carefully stir them into the mixture with the pine nuts. Butter an ovenproof dish large enough to take all the mixture. Pour it in carefully, then bake in a moderate oven (180°C, 350°F, gas mark 4) for 40 minutes. Dust with icing sugar and serve hot with single cream. The texture is not unlike that of a sponge pudding.

# FRITTELLE DI ZUCCA ALLA VENEZIANA

## VENETIAN PUMPKIN FRITTERS

You can increase or decrease the ingredients as you require for this recipe as pumpkins are usually quite large. The end result is a light and airy fritter with a lovely orange colour and an unusual flavour. Fritters are a very popular Venetian dessert and are traditionally served around Carnival time in February.

### MAKES 30

*150 g (5 oz) sultanas*
*900 g (2 lb) yellow pumpkin, peeled, seeded and cubed*
*granulated sugar*
*100 g (3¼ oz) plain flour, sifted twice*
*1 teaspoon baking powder, sifted*
*salt*
*grated rind of 1 lemon*
*oil for deep frying*

Cover the sultanas in cold water and leave to soak for 15 minutes; drain and dry. Put the pumpkin in a pan, cover with water and cook until soft; about 20 minutes. Drain it, then wrap in a cloth and squeeze out all the excess water.

Put the pumpkin in a bowl and mash it with 2 table-spoons sugar, the flour, baking powder, a large pinch of salt and the lemon rind. Stir in the sultanas. Mix it all together very thoroughly, incorporating air to make it as light and airy as possible.

Heat the oil in a deep-fat fryer to 195°C (385°F), then add walnut-sized balls of mixture and cook until crisp and golden brown. Remove with a slotted spoon and drain on kitchen paper. Sprinkle with granulated sugar and serve them as soon as the last batch has been fried. The slightly cloying taste of the pumpkin is balanced beautifully with a glass of ice cold, dry white wine.

DOVES *Three dazzlingly white doves take time to sun themselves on this pantile roof.*

# FRITTELLE

## FRITTERS WITH GRAPPA

To make these fritters you need a piping bag with a wide nozzle. The secret of success is plenty of fat to fry the fritters in. Excellent for an afternoon snack among friends.

### MAKES ABOUT 20

*200 g (7 oz) flour*
*60 g (2 oz) caster sugar*
*a pinch of salt*
*85 ml (3 fl oz) dry white wine*
*5 tablespoons grappa or a liqueur*
*30 g (1 oz) unsalted butter, melted*
*2 egg yolks, beaten*
*3 egg whites*
*oil for deep frying*
*caster sugar for dusting*

Put the flour in a bowl with the sugar and salt, and stir in the white wine, grappa, melted butter and egg yolks, to make a batter. Heat the oil in a deep-fat fryer to 195°C (385°F), so that it is waiting ready.

Whisk the egg whites until stiff and fold these into the batter. Twist the bottom of a piping bag fitted with a wide nozzle (so that the batter doesn't pour straight through) and pour the batter into it.

Standing well back, in case the fat spits, squeeze small quantities of the batter into the sizzling fat – you are aiming for a squiggly shape rather like a coil of a rope, so move the piping bag in a circular motion as you squeeze. Fry in batches of about 6 or 8. Scoop out the fritters as soon as they are crisp and brown, drain on kitchen paper and sprinkle with the sugar. Serve hot.

# SFINCIUNI DOLCI DI RISO

## SWEET SICILIAN RICE FRITTERS

The origin of these rice fritters is to be found in Sicily's Arab heritage. Apparently, one of the culinary habits in those times was to fry certain foods which had previously been allowed to ferment. These were known as 'sfinci' from which the Sicilians have derived their name for all manner of fritters – with potatoes, pumpkins, ricotta cheese and many other things. They are crisp and very crackly on the outside, with a soft inside rather like an orange rice pudding

### MAKES 18

375 ml (13 fl oz) milk
375 ml (13 fl oz) cold water
300 g (10 oz) pudding rice
grated rind of ½ a large orange
a large pinch of ground cinnamon
55 g (2 oz) caster sugar
55 g (2 oz) plain flour
7 g (¼ oz) fresh yeast, diluted in a little warm water
oil for deep frying

Mix the milk and water together and bring to the boil. As soon as they reach boiling point, add the rice and stir. Cook for about 15 minutes then leave to cool. When cold, stir in the orange rind, cinnamon, half the sugar, the flour and the yeast. Mix very thoroughly together, then set aside in a warm place, covered with a cloth, to rise for 2 hours – it doesn't puff much.

Heat the oil in a deep-fat fryer to 195°C (385°F). Using a wooden spatula and a spoon, scoop out even-sized lumps of the dough on the spatula and scrape them carefully into the hot oil with the spoon.

Fry in batches of 6 at a time until golden brown, then scoop them out with a slotted spoon and drain on kitchen paper for a few seconds before tossing lightly in the remaining sugar (you may need a little more sugar). Serve hot with icy, dry white wine.

STONE-BUILT FARM *A low group of buildings hugs the side of the hill against a sweeping panorama of receding hills.*

# PANVINESCO

## GRAPE JUICE AND SEMOLINA SWEETS

These shaped pieces of grape juice and semolina make a tasty teatime snack. Very easy and cheap to make when you have grapes growing all around you, they are always popular with adults and children. Buying 2 litres (3½ pints) grape juice is quicker, but doesn't have the same appeal as using and crushing your own grapes. If you want to make the vino cotto in advance, it can be bottled and kept in the refrigerator until you are ready to use it. You need at least 3.5 kg (8 lb) of grapes.

### MAKES ABOUT 20

*about 225 g (8 oz) fine semolina*
*coloured dragees or vermicelli, to decorate*

VINO COTTO
*4 large bunches sweet white grapes*
*4 large bunches sweet black grapes*

First make the vino cotto. Squeeze the grapes with your hands or a mouli to extract all the juice, then filter it through muslin to obtain a clear liquid. Put it into a pan (not aluminium) and boil it slowly for several hours, stirring often with a spoon until it is thick and stickily runny like honey.

Boil the vino cotto and trickle the semolina into it like a fine rain, stirring constantly to prevent lumps. When it is completely thick and lump-free, tip it out on to a marble top which has been dampened with cold water and spread it out with a spatula to a 1–3 cm (½–1¼ inch) thickness. Leave to go cold.

Cut it into different shapes with pastry cutters. Decorate with coloured dragees or vermicelli and serve 2 or 3 shapes per person. Do not store.

# DOLCE DI PANE E MELE

## BREAD AND APPLE PUDDING

From the far northern region of Alto Adige comes this delicious layered pudding of apples and bread, guaranteed to warm you on a cold day. In the summertime, use peaches or apricots instead.

### SERVES 6–8

*10 small, stale and slightly hard white breadrolls,
sliced into thin rounds
100 g (3½ oz) blanched almonds
350–500 ml (12–18 fl oz) red wine, more if required
100 g (3½ oz) granulated sugar
450 g (1 lb) apples, peeled and sliced or stoned,
unpeeled peaches or apricots
100 g (3½ oz) sultanas or currants
85 g (3 oz) unsalted butter
single cream for serving*

Prepare the bread and put it all into a bowl. Slice the almonds in half. Mix the sugar and the smaller quantity of wine and pour over the bread. Butter an ovenproof dish large enough to take all the bread and the apples.

Put a layer of wine-soaked bread on the bottom of the dish, then cover it with a layer of apple slices and a few sultanas or currants and almonds. Dot with butter, then cover with another layer of bread and fruit. Use all the ingredients in layers until you have used everything up. Make sure it is moist with plenty of wine – you can use more if you like. Dot the top generously with butter and bake in a moderate oven (180°C, 350°F, gas mark 4) for 30 minutes. Serve warm accompanied by cream.

GRAPE HARVESTING *These women are harvesting table grapes, which grow high up on the vine and must be handled with extra care.*

# PAN PEPATO

## SPICY BREAD

This is a traditional harvest time cake prepared for many centuries by the Umbrian peasants at the time when the crops were brought in. It is especially a part of the culinary scene in Spoleto and Foligno, but the tradition has spread over the border into parts of the Abruzzi and you may well find it both there and in Rome at Christmas time nowadays. The name is deceptive: it is not a bread, nor is it spicy – black pepper is the only one. Rather it's a rich flat biscuit, stuffed with nuts and chocolate, very similar to the famous Sienese panforte.

### MAKES 8 ROLLS

*55 g (2 oz) raisins
55 g (2 oz) shelled walnuts
55 g (2 oz) shelled almonds
55 g (2 oz) shelled hazelnuts
55 g (2 oz) assorted candied fruit, chopped
55 g (2 oz) cooking chocolate, chopped
a pinch of salt
a pinch of black ground pepper
4 tablespoons clear honey
3 tablespoons warm water
about 55 g (2 oz) plain flour, sifted
oil for greasing*

Cover the raisins in water and leave them to soak for 15 minutes, then drain and dry. Blanch the walnuts and the almonds in boiling water for 30 seconds, then rub off their skins. Chop them coarsely. Toast the hazelnuts in the oven for about 3 minutes and rub off their skins also. Chop and mix them with the other nuts.

Mix the candied fruit, raisins and the chocolate into the nut mixture. Add a pinch of salt and a large pinch of pepper. Dilute half the honey with the water and mix it in.

Add just enough flour to make a dough that sticks together – use as little as possible. Knead carefully, then shape it into 8 rolls. Oil and flour a baking tray, arrange the rolls on it, brush with honey and bake in a hot oven (200°C, 400°F, gas mark 6) for about 12 minutes.

PANTILE FARMHOUSE IN CHIANTI *(p 150) This Chianti farmstead nestles in the midst of extensive vineyards, cradled by wooded hills.*

# BOMBOLONI

## FLUFFY DOUGHNUTS

Mid-morning and about 6 p.m. are the times of the day when bagfuls of Bomboloni are consumed by groups of local teenagers in Tuscany. The air is filled with the sweet and irresistible scent of the doughnuts frying, and wherever you look outside the shops there are groups of young people with their mopeds, hanging about munching . . . I remember when it was Bomboloni day at home and we children were kept away from the spitting fat in the safety of the garden and would queue up outside the kitchen window waiting to be handed the hot cakes.

MAKES ABOUT 18

*450 g (1 lb) plain flour plus extra*
*115 g (4 oz) granulated sugar*
*grated rind of 1 lemon*
*½ teaspoon fine salt*
*75 g (2½ oz) softened butter*
*30 g (1 oz) fresh yeast*
*about 1.2 litres (2 pints) oil for deep frying*

Tip the flour on to the table top, add two-thirds of the sugar, the lemon rind and the salt. Shape it into a mound with your hands and plunge your fist through the centre to make a hole right down the middle.

Cut the butter into smallish pieces and put them in the hole. Knead the dry ingredients with the butter for about 5 minutes, adding just enough warm water to combine the ingredients. Crumble the yeast into a teacup and add enough warm water – about 175 ml (6 fl oz) – to make a runny, smooth paste. Add this to the dough and knead it for a further 15 minutes or until the dough is completely elastic. Put it into a lightly floured bowl, cover it with a napkin and leave to rise in a warm place for 2 hours.

Tip the dough out on to a floured surface and knead it for a couple of turns before rolling it out lightly with a rolling pin to a thickness of about 1 cm (½ inch). Using an upturned glass or a pastry cutter, cut the dough into circles. Lay large napkins or clean cloths on 2 large trays, sprinkle with flour and place the circles on the cloth without touching one another. Re-knead the trimmings,

BOMBOLONI

roll and cut into circles. Cover with a cloth and leave in a warm place for 1 hour.

Heat the oil to 180°C (350°F) in a deep-fat fryer or other suitable pan that is deeper than it is wide – there must be plenty of oil so the frying doughnuts can move around freely. When the fat is hot, add the doughnuts: put the side of the doughnut which was touching the floured cloth into the fat first. Fry about 3 at a time, rolling them over until they are puffed, golden and crisp on both sides.

Remove them with a slotted spoon and let them drain on kitchen paper, then roll them briefly in the remaining sugar. It is very important that you keep adjusting the heat under the fat so that you keep the temperature of the fat as constant and even as possible. Serve the doughnuts warm.

# BUDINO DI AVENA

## OAT PUDDING

This very simple but nourishing and comforting pudding comes from the cold northern region of Friuli. It is a pudding of Slavic origin and is perfect for children.

SERVES 6–8

*150 g (5 oz) coarse oatmeal*
*1 litre (1¾ pints) milk, or more*
*4 egg yolks*
*100 g (3½ oz) granulated sugar*
*2 tablespoons grappa or other liqueur*

Spread the oatmeal on a baking sheet and toast lightly in a oven (120°C, 225°F, gas mark ¼) for 20 minutes.

Boil the milk in a pan, sprinkle in the oatmeal, stirring continuously over low heat for 10 minutes. Press through a sieve or purée in a blender, adding a tablespoon or so of milk if needed, to make a thick cream. Return to the rinsed-out pan.

Beat the egg yolks until fluffy, add the sugar and beat for a further 5 minutes. Add to the pan and cook gently for about 7 minutes stirring constantly until it has thickened.

Dampen a pudding basin with cold water (or if it's for adults a little of your favourite liqueur) and pour in the mixture. Chill for about 4 hours, then turn out and serve.

# GESMINUS

## ORANGE BLOSSOM MERINGUES

This is an ancient Sardinian recipe handed down for many generations. They were baked briefly in a baker's oven after the bread was removed and then dried out in the sun for several days. Once these meringues were made with pure jasmine essence, but sadly this is now no longer available. They now make them with orange-flower water.

MAKES ABOUT 50

*300 g (10 oz) blanched almonds*
*oil for greasing*
*300 g (10 oz) icing sugar, sifted twice*
*4 egg whites, at room temperature*
*juice of 1 lemon*
*1 liqueur glass, 50 ml (1¾ fl oz), orange-flower water*

Line a baking sheet with greaseproof paper and oil the paper. Toast the almonds in a hot oven for about 3 minutes until golden, then slice them into long strips.

Whisk the egg whites until stiff, then whisk in the sugar to make a light dry meringue. (This is a long and tiring job, much eased by using an electric appliance!) Fold the almonds into the meringue mixture, then fold in the lemon juice and orange-flower water.

Spoon the mixture in mounds on to the baking sheet. Bake in a low oven (100°C, 200°F, gas mark low) for 2−3 hours until dry. Cool on a rack.

# PERSICATA

## SLICED PEACH SWEETMEAT

Reputedly of Persian origin, this is a lovely chewy preserve of peaches. Quinces or apples can be used.

SERVES 6−8

*1.5 kg (3 lb) ripe peaches (preferably white fleshed)*
*750 g (1½ lb) granulated or preserving sugar plus*
*sugar for sprinkling*

Blanch the peaches in boiling water for 30 seconds, then peel and remove the stones. Place them in a muslin bag to drain for 12 hours. When they have drained, weigh again − for 900 g (2 lb) of fruit you need 750 g (1½ lb) sugar. Put the fruit and sugar in a non-aluminium pan and boil, stirring constantly, until it reaches the setting stage − try a little on a plate. This takes about 1½ hours.

Pour the mixture into a shallow dish and spread it out to a depth of no more than 1−2 cm (½−¾ inch). Leave it to dry out for 7 days, preferably in a warm place, then turn it out on to a platter and sprinkle it with sugar. Cut into squares with a sharp knife and eat at once.

# TARALLI

## CALABRIAN SWEET ROLLS

These sweet rolls from Calabria contain the ever present Calabrian ingredient of honey. The longer they are left to prove, the bigger and fluffier in texture they become. They are excellent with tea or accompanying a dessert wine like Moscato, or for breakfast.

MAKES ABOUT 14

*450 g (1 lb) strong white bread flour*
*10 g (⅓ oz) fresh yeast*
*2 eggs, beaten*
*2 tablespoons olive oil*
*75 g (2½ oz) honey*

Tip the flour on to a tabletop and make a hole in the centre with your fist. Dilute the yeast with 150 ml (5 fl oz) warm water and pour into the hole. Knead together as you would a bread dough.

Leave the dough in a warm place to rise for 1 hour, then add the eggs, oil and honey and knead again. Shape the dough into about 14 figures of 8 and arrange them, well apart, on an oiled baking sheet. Leave them in a warm place to rise for up to 4 hours.

Bake them in a moderately hot oven (190°C, 375°F, gas mark 5) for about 15 minutes. Cool and store.

# GELATO DI COCOMERO

## WATERMELON ICE

The Sicilians are the masters of the art of ice cream and sorbet making. It is a skill they have learned over the centuries and which originated during the Arab occupation. The original version of this dessert was a blancmange frozen solid. Traditionally, it celebrates the Festival of the Assumption in mid-August. Various other marvellously cooling sorbets made with jasmine flowers, lemons and oranges are also prepared during the blazing summer months.

SERVES 6—8

*1 watermelon, weighing about 4.5 kg (10 lb)*
*700 g (1½ lb) caster sugar*
*4 tablespoons cornflour, sifted*
*1 teaspoon vanilla essence*
*100 g (3½ oz) cooking chocolate, chopped*
*100 g (3½ oz) candied fruit (preferably orange or pear), chopped*
*55 g (2 oz) pistachio nuts, chopped*
*ground cinnamon, to decorate*

Cut the watermelon into slices, remove all the flesh and push it through a sieve into a pan. Mix the sugar and cornflour into the watermelon, then bring to the boil and simmer for 5—6 minutes, stirring constantly. When it has thickened, add the vanilla essence.

Pour the mixture into a dampened mould and freeze until mushy enough to support the additions. Beat to break up the ice crystals, then fold in the chopped chocolate, candied fruit and nuts. Freeze in 6—8 dampened moulds, or one big mould. Turn out and decorate with a little cinnamon before serving.

# CROSTATA DI MANDORLE

## ALMOND TART

This is a delightfully simple and delicious almond tart with the filling sandwiched inside. Perfect for breakfast or for tea, its dry dense texture is designed to accompany drinks of some sort.

This is another sweet, with its sugar and almonds, that came from the Arabs. Indeed Italian desserts divide into those that are plain by modern standards, and ones that betray an Eastern influence and are very sugary.

SERVES 8—10

*450 g (1 lb) ground almonds*
*225 g (8 oz) caster sugar*
*225 g (8 oz) plain flour*
*grated rind ½ a lemon*
*3 egg whites*
*5 egg yolks*
*2 eggs*
*a pinch of ground cinnamon*
*a pinch of ground cloves*
*butter for greasing*

Mix half the ground almonds, half the sugar, the flour and lemon rind. Add the egg whites, kneading them in to make a rather stiff dough. In a separate bowl, mix together the remaining ground almonds, sugar and the spices. Beat the egg yolks and whole eggs and add, then mix to a smooth creamy texture.

Grease a 25 cm (10 inch) flan tin with butter and roll out the dough to make 2 even-sized circles to fit the tin. Lay the first circle on the bottom of the tin and spread the filling on the top. Lay the second circle over it, pinch the edges tightly closed all around, then bake in a moderate oven (180°C, 350°F, gas mark 4) for 30—40 minutes. Serve cool.

# GNOCCHI DOLCI DI NATALE

## SWEET CHRISTMAS GNOCCHI

This is my own variation of the most ancient and traditional dish for an Umbrian Christmas. It calls for pasta to be cut into squares, boiled, then dressed with the walnut mixture and eaten cold. I don't like cold pasta at the best of times – especially not when it's sweet and chocolatey – but the walnut mixture is so good and easy to make that I decided to use it in this way instead. Serve with chilled Vin Santo as an unusual end to a Christmas feast.

SERVES 8–10

*50 walnuts*
*150 g (5 oz) granulated sugar*
*1 tablespoon white breadcrumbs*
*50 g (1¾ oz) bitter cooking chocolate, grated*
*grated rind of ½ lemon*
*1 liqueur glass sweet liqueur*
*a large pinch of ground cinnamon*
*about 4 tablespoons milk, if necessary*
*450 g (1 lb) plain flour*
*1 egg*
*oil for deep frying*
*icing sugar for dusting*

Crack open the nuts, blanch them in boiling water, then peel. Put them in a food processor with the sugar, breadcrumbs, chocolate, lemon rind, liqueur and cinnamon. If the mixture is very stiff, thin with a little milk.

Mix together the flour, egg and as much warm water as needed to make a smooth dough. Knead thoroughly for about 15 minutes.

Roll out the dough as thinly as possible: this is important and a pasta machine would help. Cut into 4 cm (1¾ inch) squares and brush round the edge with water. Place a little of the walnut filling in the centre of each one, fold in half and press closed tightly. Heat the oil in a deep-fat fryer, to 195°C (385°F). Add the pasta, about 4 at a time, rolling them over with a slotted spoon until they are crisp and golden brown. Drain on kitchen paper and dust with icing sugar. Serve hot or cold.

# GNOCCHI DOLCI DI LATTE

## SWEET MILKY DUMPLINGS

This is a delicately flavoured and delicious pudding, which is nevertheless very substantial. It is a great comfort food for anybody but is particularly good for old people, convalescing invalids and children as it has a very slippery texture.

SERVES 4–6

*500 ml (18 fl oz) milk*
*3 egg yolks*
*50 g (1¾ oz) sugar*
*75 g (2½ oz) cornflour*
*2 large pinches of ground cinnamon*
*a pinch of salt*
*2 tablespoons freshly grated Parmesan cheese*
*30 g (1 oz) butter, melted*

Heat the milk to boiling point. Beat the egg yolks in an enamelled or other flameproof non-aluminium bowl with about half the sugar, the cornflour, a pinch of cinnamon and salt. Mix carefully together, adding the milk a little at a time. Stir this mixture into a smooth, thick cream over a very low heat.

When the cornflour has thickened completely, pour the cream out on to an ovenproof dish so that it is 1 cm (½ inch) deep.

Scatter the Parmesan cheese, a pinch of cinnamon and the remaining sugar over the top and drizzle with the melted butter. Bake in a moderate oven (180°C, 350°F, gas mark 4) for 10 minutes. Leave to rest, out of the oven, for a further 10 minutes before cutting into cubes to serve.

WINDOW IN ASSISI *For much of the year, windows are left wide open, so the people indoors can enjoy fresh air and the scent of the flowers.*

# INDEX

*Note:* Recipes and ingredients are generally indexed under their English titles. Illustrations are not indexed.

# ACKNOWLEDGMENTS

The publisher thanks the following photographers and organizations for their kind permission to reproduce the photographs in this book:

1 Pierre Hussenot/Agence Top; 2 Monica Fiore/Fiorepress; 3 John G Ross/Landscape Only; 6–7 Charlie Waite/Landscape Only; 8 Anthony Blake Photo Library; 22 John G Ross/Landscape Only; 24–25 Brian Harris/Impact Photos; 27 Guy Bouchet; 30 Anthony Blake Photo Library; 32 Riccardo Villarose/Explorer; 241 Anthony Blake Photo Library; 42–43 Gary Rogers; 44–45 P. Curto/Marka; 47 Jacqueline Guillot/Agence Top; 50 Christian Errath/Explorer; 55 Anthony Blake Photo Library; 57 John G Ross/Robert Harding Picture Library; 63 A Faulkner-Taylor/Robert Harding Picture Library; 64 Bullaty/Lomeo/The Image Bank; 66 Serge Chirol; 72–73 Fuirepress; 74–75 Zefa Picture Library; 76 Guy Bouchet; 84–85 Fiore/Explorer; 86–87 Pierre Putelat/Agence Top; 90 Zefa Picture Library; 92–93 Will McBride/The Image Bank; 96 Zefa Picture Library; 103 Liba Taylor/Hutchison Library; 104 Guy Bouchet; 106–107 L Coccia/Marka; 108 Guy Bouchet; 109 John G Ross/Robert Harding Picture Library; 114 Alex Dufort/Impact Photos; 118–119 Marcella Pedone/ The Image Bank; 125 Christine Tiberghien; 126–127 Marka; 128 Christine Fleurent/Agence Top; 129 Guy Bouchet; 133 Marka; 140 de Gex/Hutchison Library; 144 G Buntrock/Anthony Blake Photo Library; 146–147 Serge Chirol; 148 Donatello Brogioni/Grazia Neri; 150–151 Zefa Picture Library; 156 Zefa Picture Library. Special photography by Linda Burgess: 18–19, 28–29, 35, 36–37, 48–49, 52–53, 58–59, 69, 78–79, 80–81, 88–89, 95, 98–99, 112–113, 117, 120–121, 130–131, 134, 136–137, 142–143, 152.

Thanks to

The Criterion Tile Shop
196 Wandsworth Bridge Rd
London SW6 2UF

Fired Earth Tiles
37–41 Battersea High St
London SW11 3JF

Judy & Tony
293 Westbourne Grove
London W11

Lunn Antiques
86 New Kings Rd
London SW6

Richard Dare
93 Regents Park Rd
London NW1

Ann Lingard
Rope Walk Antiques
Rye
Sussex

Stitches & Daughters
Blackheath Village
London SE3

Tobias & The Angel
68 White Hart Lane
Barnes
London SW13

The Dining Room Shop
62/64 White Hart Lane
Barnes
London SW13

The Gallery of Antique
Costume & Textiles
22 Church St
London NW8

The Conran Shop
Fulham Rd
London SW3

J K Hill
Handmade Pottery
151 Fulham Rd
London SW3